The Power of Dark Psychology and Influence

(2 in 1)

11 Secrets to Understand People's Minds, Build Unbreakable Trust, and Lead Others With Ease.

HALBERT WARD

© Copyright 2024 - All rights reserved.

The content inside this book may not be duplicated, reproduced, or transmitted without direct written permission from the author or publisher.

Under no circumstances will any blame or legal responsibility be held against the publisher, or author, for any damages, reparation, or monetary loss due to the information contained within this book, either directly or indirectly.

Legal Notice:

This book is copyright protected. It is only for personal use. You cannot amend, distribute, sell, use, quote or paraphrase any part, or the content within this book, without the consent of the author or publisher.

Disclaimer Notice:

Please note the information contained within this document is for educational and entertainment purposes only. All effort has been executed to present accurate, reliable, up to date, complete information. No warranties of any kind are declared or implied. Readers acknowledge that the author is not engaging in the rendering of legal, financial, medical, or professional advice. The content within this book has been derived from various sources. Please consult a licensed professional before attempting any techniques outlined in this book.

By reading this document, the reader agrees that under no circumstances is the author responsible for any losses, direct or indirect, that are incurred as a result of the use of the information contained within this document, including, but not limited to, errors, omissions, or inaccuracies.

TABLE OF CONTENT

Dark Psychology 1.0

11 Hidden Influential Powers

DARK PSYCHOLOGY 1.0

MASTER THE SECRETS SCIENCE OF SILENT DOMINATION, SUBCONSCIOUS INFLUENCE, AND UNSEEN BEHAVIORAL CONTROL TECHNIQUES.

HALBERT WARD

CHAPTER 1
Introduction To Dark Psychology

Dark Psychology is an area that is often disregarded in the dimly illuminated corridors of the human psyche, where ideas echo and sentiments swirl in shadowy recesses of consciousness. Hi there, brave reader. Welcome to an exciting journey where you will learn about the mysterious science, the dark arts, and the puppeteer of behavior control that lies behind quiet dominance, subconscious control, and subliminal influence.

As we embark on this voyage into the depths of the human mind, get ready to have your preconceptions debunked and deepen your comprehension of the covert strategies that have impacted politics, history, and interpersonal relationships. Dark Psychology is more than a book; it explores our unconscious minds, a labyrinthine place where forces beyond our comprehension shape our lives.

In this domain, quiet is more than just the lack of sound; quiet is a potent tool and preferred weapon for those who know how to exercise subtle influence. Imagine living in a world where actions speak louder than words and subtle comments have more weight than articulate ones. Unravel the mysterious language of quiet domination in Dark Psychology to uncover the threads that crisscross human behavior.

But our journey doesn't finish here—rather, it continues in the subconscious, where puppeteers with genuine impact operate. As we investigate this psychic maze, we will reveal how unseen forces shape our decisions, desires, and destiny. Prepare to explore the world of subconscious influence, where the mind is the battlefield and the winning strategy.

The following pages will not only make the unclear apparent but also arm you with the information you need to navigate the intricate dance of behavioral regulation. By using the techniques covered in this book, you will be able to recognize the forces at play and develop the skills necessary to either effectively use them or resist them. It will feel as though you have an unseen hand guiding you.

If you're ready to answer the riddles, challenge the established wisdom, and delve into the depths of the human psyche, turn the page now. I promise this book to read if you're ready to delve deeper, understand, and solve the riddles that lie under the surface. From this point on, your journey will reveal that you are not just reading a book; rather, you are unlocking doors to a universe in which the keys to power are found in the mysteries of psychology. I'd also want you to follow the details closely as we will build the following chapters upon previous chapters. Salutations and salutations on this initiation.

THE MEANING OF DARK PSYCHOLOGY.

Dark psychology is one area of psychology that stands out as both fascinating and occasionally scary. Let's dissect its true meaning so that you can comprehend it.

Dark psychology explores the hidden intricacies beneath human relationships and motivations, not the celebration of damage. It investigates techniques for dominating, influencing, and controlling the subconscious. In contrast to conventional psychology, which emphasizes the positive elements of conduct, Dark Psychology illuminates the dubious domains of coercion, persuasion, and manipulation. It recognizes that to comprehend human behavior completely, we must also understand its darker aspects.

Consider Dark Psychology as a mirror reflecting the hidden forces influencing our behavior and ideas. It employs a range of strategies, from more covert manipulation to subtly persuading, and provides insight into the factors that have shaped society, history, and interpersonal relationships.

Dark psychology is the art of silent communication or persuasion without outright conflict. It uses nonverbal clues to illuminate a world where deeds speak louder than words. Being conscious of this subtle effect enables one to move through social environments with more awareness.

Furthermore, Dark Psychology explores the subconscious mind, the site of influence. It exposes the invisible puppets influencing attitudes and aspirations. We can see the invisible factors influencing conduct by comprehending subconscious impact.

THE DEVELOPMENT OF DARK PSYCHOLOGY.

Dark psychology has developed throughout time, characterized by gradual changes in human perception and the identification of complex patterns woven across the web of covert behavioral control, subconscious influence, and silent dominance. We find ourselves following in the footsteps of those who ventured into the murky corners of the human psyche as we delve deeper into the development of Dark Psychology.

1. Historical Origins of Dark Psychology:

Dark psychology has historical roots that date back to a time when political and social dynamics heavily relied on manipulation and power conflicts. The ability to subdue people subtly was demonstrated by the political maneuvers of the ancient empires, when strategic influence was pivotal in determining the course of entire civilizations.

To fully grasp Dark Psychology, we must examine these early examples of influence and control and see how they prepared the ground for the emergence of this fascinating science. Early examples of persuasion and control are like essential threads in the historical tapestry that weave the fabric of Dark Psychology. Consider the political environments of the past empires, where leaders used the implicit art of dominance as a tactical weapon.

Rulers and strategists used cunning strategies to control people around them in the enormous corridors of power. These skilled manipulators knew that overt assertions of power might provoke resistance or insurrection. Rather, they became experts at silent dominance, using complex networks of sway to sway the thoughts and choices of those vital to their rule.

The political intrigue that existed throughout the Roman Empire is one prominent example. Leaders such as Augustus and Julius Caesar were adept at psychological manipulation in addition to military strategy. In an era of political unpredictability, they learned how to maintain stability by controlling important persons within their inner circles through alliances, fear, and loyalty.

Similarly, the Qin Dynasty's idea of "Legalism" emphasized rigorous regulation and the strategic use of terror to uphold order in ancient China. Legalist philosophers understood that the psychological effect of fear might stifle disagreement and reinforce authority, which is why they promoted severe penalties and a distinct hierarchy.

Another early example is the Mauryan Empire, led by Chandragupta Maurya, which extended eastward to the Indian subcontinent. The "Arthashastra," a book on statecraft and strategy that explored the psychological aspects of government, was written by Chanakya, the advisor of Chandragupta. It described strategies for maintaining political control through espionage, deceit, and even assassination.

These historical examples highlight the early origins of Dark Psychology when influential people realized how effective subtle influence might be in preserving power. The insights gained from these experiences paved the way for dark psychology to develop into a complex theory that explains the complex interplay between control, power, and the human psyche.

2. Machiavellian Tricks: Deciphering Gothic Psychology in Renaissance Art.

The Renaissance saw the application of Dark Psychology principles prominently in Niccolò Machiavelli's influential writings, especially in his well-known work "The Prince." Machiavelli's exploration of political scheming and manipulation during this time established key tenets of Dark Psychology and provided a strong framework for comprehending the more complex aspects of human nature.

Machiavelli explores duplicity and pragmatic power in "The Prince" without holding back. His candid admission of these strategies was a turning point in the evolution of Dark Psychology as a separate field of study. Machiavelli essentially exposed the hard truth that sometimes, using tactics that appear morally dubious is necessary for the quest and preservation of power.

Because it emphasizes the value of strategic manipulation in achieving desired results, Machiavelli's writings have become a valuable resource for leaders navigating the intricate web of politics. Dark Psychology thus crystallized throughout the Renaissance, as Machiavelli's insights on the strategic use of power and manipulation had a lasting impression on the developing understanding of human behavior.

During this period, I served as a link between the political intrigues of antiquity and the emerging field of Dark Psychology, proving that psychological manipulation and quiet influence were useful techniques and essential tools for anyone looking to comprehend and use power in a sophisticated way.

3. Introducing Freudian Shadows: A Look at Dark Psychology in the Early 1900s.

With the advent of the early 20th century, Sigmund Freud's seminal work sets the psychological framework for Dark Psychology. His research into the subconscious mind gave the field a fresh perspective. By illuminating the hidden worlds of impulses, desires, and the unconscious forces that subtly shape human conduct, Freud's work was like having a flashlight shined on it. This psychoanalytic viewpoint contributed significantly to the development of Dark Psychology by deepening our understanding of the invisible forces at work beneath the surface.

The theories of Freud become essential to comprehending the shadows that influence our thoughts and behavior. His focus on the unconscious mind as a storehouse of repressed motives and desires struck a chord with the fundamental ideas of Dark Psychology, illuminating the complex web of influences that frequently elude conscious awareness.

Freud's insights gave Dark Psychology a theoretical foundation and helped us comprehend how our subconscious minds became arenas for influences and impulses. This period was crucial in the evolution of dark psychology because it combined a deeper investigation of the dark corners of the human mind with historical roots and Machiavellian influences.

4. Behavioral Psychology: Illuminating Negative Psychology in the Mid-20th Cent.

Behavioral psychology gains prominence as the 20th century ends, providing a scientific lens through which to examine the workings of behavior modification. In this area, which examined training, reinforcement, and the manipulation of stimuli to affect behavior in people, dark psychology found a warm and accepting home. This era solidified the real-world applications of dark psychology concepts by moving beyond idle conjecture to explore theories actively through experiments.

In essence, behavioral psychology evolved into a research lab for comprehending how outside influences could mold and regulate behavior. Scholars investigated the potential for systematically employing rewards, punishments, and environmental clues to steer individuals toward specific behaviors. This scientific perspective not only increased the level of accuracy in the study of Dark Psychology but also made it possible to apply Dark Psychology to a variety of real-world situations.

The concentration on empirical research throughout the mid-20th century served as a link between Dark Psychology's theoretical underpinnings and practical applications. During this crucial period, the skill of subtly influencing behavior transitioned from theoretical concepts to concrete tests and applications, thereby reinforcing Dark Psychology as a science with quantifiable and useful aspects.

5. Dark psychology and social psychology: integrating the two fields.

Dark psychology became a part of social psychology as the social sciences developed. Here, the emphasis switched to comprehending social influence, conformity, and group dynamics, illuminating how societal currents could subtly guide people. Within this framework, Dark Psychology emerged as a crucial component for understanding the intricate interactions between personal conduct and the broader social dynamics.

In a sense, social psychology became a platform for the larger-scale application of Dark Psychology ideas. Researchers looked at how individuals follow social norms, adjust to cultural expectations, and are impacted by the prevalent views in their communities. It became clear that the deceptive influence and manipulation covered in Dark Psychology went beyond one-on-one encounters to the larger framework of social systems.

Dark psychology emerged as a key concept in this era of understanding how society is shaped by collective behaviors as much as by individual acts. It cemented its place as a crucial component of the changing field of social psychology by offering us a prism to understand how societal factors influence our ideas, choices, and behaviors.

6. Dark psychology in the era of technology is an influence.

Technology has created new opportunities for Dark Psychology to reveal its strategies in the modern world. Unseen influencers use the digital landscape as a bright playground to discreetly shape people's views and behaviors on a vast scale. Technology has become a major factor driving Dark Psychology's modernization and evolution due to the complexity of social media dynamics and the data-driven techniques used in many industries.

In particular, the emergence of social media has given rise to a fertile field for subtle impacts. Our online experiences are guided by algorithms and targeted content manipulation behind the scenes, which affects what we view, like, and share. Here is where Dark Psychology's unseen hands are at work, trying to manipulate our digital relationships in ways that aren't necessarily obvious.

Furthermore, the strategic use of data has emerged as a key player in influencing customer behavior across various businesses. Businesses use complex algorithms to forecast consumer preferences and customize their marketing approaches. This data-driven strategy is a modern example of Dark Psychology, in which information is manipulated to influence our choices and behaviors—often without our knowledge.

Dark Psychology has expanded its impact and reached this new chapter marked by the modern era. In this environment, the quiet influencers work in the digital shadows, using technology as a catalyst to create previously unheard-of-scale networks of subtle influence.

7. Current Applications: The Use of Dark Psychology in a Variety of Sectors.

Dark psychology is now actively being used in several real-world contexts, moving beyond simple theories. The ideas of Dark Psychology are actively influencing the landscape of influence, whether in the strategic domains of marketing, the complex terrain of politics, or the fragile fabric of interpersonal relationships. The skills of persuasion, manipulation, and subtle dominance are still valuable in the modern world because they can adjust to the constantly shifting dynamics of our interconnected society.

Businesses apply the ideas of Dark Psychology to marketing to sway consumer choices. The intention behind everything from skillfully designed commercials to deceptive product placements is to influence perceptions and direct customer behavior without the consumer even recognizing it. Businesses use psychological strategies to make their products more enticing; it's a deliberate dance.

The game of influence is paramount in politics. Political leaders use a variety of Dark Psychology tactics, such as influencing public opinion and employing persuasive communication methods. The goal is frequently to gently sway the electorate's attitudes in favor of particular policies or politicians without making the deceptive methods used obvious.

It is possible to see aspects of Dark Psychology even in casual interactions. People use strategies of influence, whether they are aware of it or not, in everything from the delicate power dynamics in families to the complications of friendships. Understanding these dynamics can enable people to negotiate relationships with greater awareness because it's a part of the social fabric.

In summary, Dark Psychology has evolved into a useful instrument that can be applied to various sectors to meet the complicated needs of our contemporary, globalized society. It's not limited to talks in academic settings; it actively shapes how companies sell their goods, politicians sway public opinion, and people move through the delicate dance of influence in daily life.

As we follow the evolution of Dark Psychology, it becomes clear that its roots are profound and its branches extensive. This investigation is not merely a historical look back; rather, it is an acknowledgment that the concepts of subliminal influence, behavioral control, and quiet dominance continue to exist and evolve in response to the dynamic environment of human interaction. We shall analyze these events in the following paragraphs, revealing the mysteries that have withstood the test of time and continue to influence the invisible forces that control our existence.

THE COMPLEXITIES OF MANIPULATIVE SCIENCES.

Upon delving into the historical foundations and developmental trajectory of Dark Psychology, we will unavoidably come across the vast network of nuances ingrained in the manipulative sciences. This investigation goes beyond the significant historical moments to examine the subtleties, difficulties, and complex aspects that characterize the current state of silent dominance, subconscious influence, and behavioral control. It includes the following:

1. The Interaction of Historical Underpinnings: Dissecting the Origins of Deception.

The historical underpinnings we have unearthed are intricately intertwined with the convoluted pathways of manipulative sciences. Each historical period has contributed unique strands to the complex fabric of Dark Psychology, influencing its development and molding its instruments of control. Comprehending the interaction of historical effects is essential to understanding the complex dynamics that characterize the manipulative sciences of today.

Consider it as the process of removing layers from a historical onion. Every historical period made an impact and added crucial components to the always-changing story of Dark Psychology, from the political intrigues of ancient empires to the crafty methods of Niccol Machiavelli. Dark psychology developed and expanded because of the early foundations, the Renaissance's crystallization of ideas, Freudian insights into the subconscious, Behavioral Psychology's experimentation, and Social Psychology's study of group dynamics.

Comprehending the historical interplay is a road map for navigating the complex world of manipulative sciences. It gives us the background information we need to make the connections between earlier influences and more recent expressions. The historical linkages molded the ideas and the application of these deceptive strategies in our tech-driven, contemporary environment.

Therefore, understanding the historical interplay between the manipulative sciences aids in our ability to unravel complex patterns and show how the instruments of influence have changed over time. It explores the historical echoes that continue to reverberate in the present, leading us to understand the intricate network of Dark Psychology that permeates our modern world.

2. Navigating the Manipulative Sciences in the 21st Century: Adaptation in the Digital Age.

In the twenty-first century, manipulative sciences have easily adapted to the digital era. As previously mentioned, the impact of the digital age marks a significant turning point that brings new difficulties and dimensions. In response, Dark Psychology has embraced the complexities and opportunities the digital sphere offers.

Algorithmic persuasion has emerged as a prominent participant in the huge field of social media. Algorithms work in the background, analyzing our online activity and customizing content to catch our eye and gently sway our opinions. It works in the shadows of our online experiences, akin to a digital puppeteer directing what we read, watch, and interact with.

Dark Psychology has also established itself in the individualized aspect of internet advertising. Advertisers employ data-driven techniques to target particular audiences and get insight into individual preferences. As a result, advertisements are customized for every user, appealing to their unique interests and wants in a way that can be almost uncanny.

This digital age adaption is a tactical move to take advantage of the internet world's enormous reach and a reaction to technology improvements. Dark psychology has become pervasive in modern digital interactions, affecting our decisions and reshaping our online experiences in ways we may not even be aware of. It is no longer limited to traditional settings.

The manipulative sciences have developed to flourish in the digital era by using technology effectively. Dark psychology is a dance of influence in the linked domains of social media, algorithms, and personalized information, which keeps changing and adding to the ever-evolving fabric of human behavior.

3. Adaptation in the Digital Age: Handling Deception in the Virtual Environment.

The art of manipulation has seamlessly moved to the digital age in the twenty-first century. As we previously discussed, technology has introduced new obstacles and new methods. In response, Dark Psychology has welcomed the opportunities and challenges the digital age presents.

There's a phenomenon on social media known as algorithmic persuasion. It functions like a backstage director, observing your online activities and presenting you with content that it believes would appeal to you or influence your opinion. It resembles having a puppeteer manipulating your internet experiences invisibly over what you see and do.

Then, online advertisements appear to be highly aware of your preferences. Advertisers employ cunning tactics to determine your interests and present you with adverts they believe will catch your eye. It resembles receiving tailored advertisements that specifically target your interests and preferences.

This adaptation to the digital age can be seen as a reaction to how technology has altered society. Dark psychology is now present online as well as in more conventional settings. It shapes what we see and influences our decisions behind social media scenes and targeted advertisements, frequently without our awareness.

Put, manipulation techniques have evolved to suit our virtual world. They're influencing our decisions and actions online by wielding technology as a potent tool. In the age of social media, algorithms, and tailored content, Dark Psychology is keeping up and leaving its mark on our online behavior. It's like a dance of influence.

4. Striking the Correct Balance: Your Ability vs. Potential Tricks.

Let's start on a challenging task: finding the balance between feeling powerful and resisting manipulations. Understanding Dark Psychology can help you recognize manipulation and take action to prevent it. But here's the thing: being aware of these tactics increases the likelihood that you could be the victim of one of them. This delicate balancing act prompts us to consider awareness, education, and the responsible application of this complex knowledge.

5. Defying Tricks with Strength: Developing Mental Resilience.

Speaking of managing difficult material, let's discuss the complexities of manipulative sciences. It's critical to pay attention to psychological resiliency. This entails determining how people might fortify themselves against deceptive kinds of influence. Navigating the twists and turns of manipulative sciences requires helping people recognize where they can be vulnerable, recognize cunning strategies, and fortify their mental barriers.

6. New Discoveries in Brain Science: Navigating the Unknown in Manipulative Sciences.

Here's the twist: the field of manipulative sciences is becoming even more complex due to advancements in brain science. Understanding how the brain reacts to various stimuli presents new possibilities and obstacles. Dark psychology and brain science explore uncharted territory by examining how our biology may render us more manipulable. It's like venturing into uncharted territory where we may uncover hints as to why we react to deceptive stimuli as we do.

It is clear from studying the intricacies of the manipulative sciences that this research is dynamic. The field is still developing, bringing new difficulties and moral dilemmas. Our voyage delves into historical underpinnings and current challenges, allowing readers to understand the nuances that shape the field of dark psychology in the modern period. Welcome to the core of the manipulative sciences, where traversing the shadows requires an awareness of the complexity.

Even though we have already completed the first chapter of "Dark Psychology 1.0," our investigation into the shadows is far from over. We've examined the complexities of manipulative sciences, including their historical underpinnings, digital era adaptation, ethical dilemmas, personal grit, mental toughness, and uncharted territory in neuroscience. However, there's a great eagerness in the air—a wish to delve even farther into the history of the covert power that we've only just begun to unravel.

Imagine yourself at a crossroads in history, looking back to the period when manipulation first raised its enigmatic shadow. In the upcoming chapter, we'll embark on a fascinating historical voyage to examine the first uses of quiet control techniques. It's not merely a retrospective but an intriguing investigation into the foundations that securely establish Dark Psychology in the human condition.

We'll turn the pages of time to uncover the origins of quiet control, from the covert strategies employed by early leaders to the deftly nimble manipulation laced into historical tales. Every turn of the historical page reveals another dimension, an untold tale, or a pivotal event that influenced Dark Psychology.

Prepare to see the emergence of tactics that impacted politics, empires, and interpersonal relationships. You'll delve into a centuries-spanning tale as we examine the beginnings of Dark Psychology, connecting cunning tactics, profound psychological understanding, and the subliminal murmurs of authority reverberating across time.

The first examples of silent control techniques are not merely historical anecdotes; they serve as the cornerstone upon which manipulative sciences have developed and evolved. The strategies of influence that have molded our interactions will be revealed in the upcoming chapter as we unearth secrets stashed away in old scrolls.

So, my dear reader, as we close this first chapter, I cordially ask you to turn the page and follow me into the manipulative historical maze. Awaiting you is Chapter Two, which promises a fascinating investigation into the origin of Dark Psychology. It's a voyage that will captivate your imagination, test your assumptions, and unveil the secrets at the heart of silent control.

CHAPTER 2
The Origin Of Dark Psychology

Dark Psychology sneaked in years ago, back when whispers could carry great power and darkness hid the craft of manipulation. Imagine yourself amid intrigue and the quiet sharing of secrets in an old royal court. We reveal the mysterious origins of Dark Psychology here in the center of history—a fascinating voyage that spans the ages.

A maestro of silent control, whose cunning maneuvers dictated the fates of entire nations, appears amid the beauty of former empires. Come to the bygone era's royal courts, where incense and whispers of power coexisted and deft movements subdued monarchs and conquerors.

This first chapter of Dark Psychology's Origins takes us beyond historical details and into stories intertwined with the strands of subliminal power. Get ready to hear tales of psychological shadows, sly intrigue, and time-tested tactics that have resonated throughout history. Every thread in the old tapestry tells a story as we enter, revealing the mysteries that paved the way for the manipulating sciences we study today.

As you read this, my reader, prepare for a trip through time where the dance of manipulation takes place against the majestic backdrops of dynasties and empires. The beginnings of Dark Psychology are more than just historical teachings; they are windows into a time when power was vested in the delicate skill of manipulation. In the future, tales of strategic prowess will animate the pages, unveiling the ageless foundations from which Dark Psychology originated. Welcome to Chapter Two, when the past takes center stage, and the roots of silent control are ingrained in time.

HISTORICAL LOOK AT MANIPULATION.

Imagine yourself strolling through the passageways of time, where the subtle threads of influence weave through the pages of human history, and the echoes of the past linger. You are encouraged to explore the rich tapestry of manipulation in this chapter. Each historical era opens up like a chapter as we unroll this historical scroll, revealing the strategies, plots, and subtle manipulations that have shaped the course of entire civilizations. So, let's dive right into the manipulation points throughout history.

1. Ancient Mesopotamia: The Cradle of Silent Scheming.

There was a subtle game of manipulation long ago in Mesopotamia, the birthplace of civilization. Everything happened in the region between the Tigris and Euphrates rivers, particularly in Ur and Babylon. These cities' leaders were adept at manipulating politics. They could dance like pros and left a lasting pattern of impact. The foundations of a quiet but powerful sort of power were painstakingly laid in Ur and Babylon.

They discovered that maintaining control required forging wise relationships. Thus, these leaders engaged in backroom negotiations and bargains to maintain dominance. However, it was more than politics; it was also a display of allegiance. Leaders could project an image of strength and commitment that inspires confidence in others. This action was calculated to maintain solid support, not merely for show.

If Mesopotamia were a massive chessboard, these leaders would be the pieces moving strategically—every choice they made influenced history, creating a lasting impression. The legacy of this silent plotting began to take shape as the sun sank below the Tigris and Euphrates. A sophisticated and powerful style of politics emerged in Mesopotamia, the birthplace of civilization, and it helped shape the way power was distributed for centuries to come.

2. Temples in Egypt: Mythical Cords of Influence.

A fascinating story was told in the great temples of Egypt. Mysticism was the secret instrument used by priests and scribes to create a tapestry of influence, much like a skillful weaver. This silent authority was attained by mysterious rituals, symbols, and profound understanding rather than force.

Consider the scribes and priests as storytellers who performed enigmatic rites essential to influencing spirituality. They employed a subdued dance of manipulation that worked on a different plane rather than yelling their dominance. These were not ceremonial rites. Every gesture and symbol had a deep significance, and their understanding of the magical arts served as a map to an otherworldly realm. The scribes and priests were skilled at instilling awe and reverence in the populace by employing this mysticism.

Imagine now the shadows cast by the great pyramids, observing this singular fusion of subtle domination and mysticism as it happened. It was more than just a show of strength; it was a merging of the quiet and the spiritual, making a profound mark on the annals of antiquity. A silent symphony of influence was being orchestrated amid the luxury of the Egyptian temples by priests and scribes skilled at assimilating mysticism into the fabric of authority. This supernatural influence's legacy reverberated across time, permanently altering the ancient world.

3. Greek City-States: The Convincing Symphony of the Agora.

An intriguing play occurred in the bustling agora, the marketplace of classical Greece. This was no typical market; instead, it was a venue where persuasion was king. Prominent philosophers and orators, such as the well-known Sophists, came into prominence and used rhetoric—the deft use of language—as a potent instrument to influence public opinion.

Let's focus on these philosophers and orators now. Specifically, the Sophists resembled the superstars of persuasion. They were masters in persuasion and could change people's minds with their words. Imagine them as persuasive speakers who could simplify and convincingly convey even the most difficult concepts.

The Greek city-states evolved from being merely geographical places to become settings for this subtly manipulative power struggle. Think of these city-states as theaters and rhetoric as the well-crafted and delivered screenplay meant to enthrall the people in the audience. The agora was a vibrant center of ideas rather than just a location to purchase and sell goods. Imagine individuals congregating to discuss and have debates in addition to exchanging commodities. It was a whirlwind of ideas and perspectives. Thus, amid this dynamic blend of rhetorical prowess and philosophical debates, the Greek city-states were testing grounds for the development of manipulation science. It was not about using force but rather about the skill of persuasion, leaving a legacy that would affect politics and philosophy across the Hellenic world.

4. Political ballet and harmony in the Chinese dynasties.

A fascinating story was being told in the tranquil courts of ancient China. It was more than just leaders giving commands; it was a ballet of political intrigue and harmony. See the emperors and courtiers as artists on a magnificent stage, participating in a nuanced ballet in which each step had a purpose.

Words were one of many means of communication in Chinese courts. A nod or a small movement could say more than words in this silent language of gestures. This silent dialogue developed into an essential component of the political dance.

Let's now concentrate on symbolic presents. These were more than just gifts; they were very symbolic messages. Every present served a purpose: to show loyalty, form alliances, or occasionally even to issue a warning quietly. Without saying a word, the strategic game of symbol trading communicated a lot.

Remember to be wary of disguised threats as well. Imagine this as a game of chess when threats are made subtly rather than outright. Comparable to a calculated play on a political chessboard, it hinted at outcomes without saying them out loud.

Chinese dynasties employed silent dominance methods akin to a skillfully performed ballet, aiming to strike a balance between upholding political control and preserving harmony within the court. It was more than just governing; it was a kind of politics where the delicate idea of harmony was combined with the elaborate movements of a political ballet. This dance, performed in ancient Chinese courts, is remembered forever in the annals of history.

5. Roman Senate: The Powerful Silent Schemes:

An enthralling tale took place within the Roman Senate's august chambers. This was more than just a forum for conversation; it was a platform for the silent exercise of power. Consider the senators as accomplished participants in a political dance that transcended heated arguments.

Let's now explore delicate coalitions. Senators acted as architects, constructing bridges of mutual respect and interest. It involved more than just exchanging viewpoints; it involved developing ties behind the scenes to support each other's beliefs. Imagine this as a carefully crafted network of relationships.

Subsequently, there existed tactical unions. These were strategic unions to forge alliances and assemble power rather than love tales. Senators were aware of the power of familial relationships in politics, and they saw marriages as contracts that shaped politics and personal life.

Consider instances of faithfulness. Senators demonstrated their loyalty in calculated ways rather than just stating it. Every move was calculated to show loyalty and win over other senators and the public, much like in a chess match.

These senators were experts at political scheming in the center of the Roman Republic, setting the foundation for the practice of subdued power. Their subdued schemes had an impact inside the Senate and throughout Rome's history, influencing the development of one of the most powerful civilizations in antiquity.

6. Mediaeval Courts: The Trickery Dance.

A captivating drama emerges as we join the medieval courts of Europe, with the dance of deception taking center stage. Imagine a world of castles and knights, where aristocrats and kings were adept manipulators and rulers. In this age of gallantry and betrayal, the art of deceit became a skill that the powerful honed.

Let's now discuss coded language. It mattered not just what was said but also how it was told. To convey plans and strategies, nobility and monarchs created secret language by employing words with concealed connotations. It resembled having a code language only people with inside knowledge could comprehend.

A key element of this medieval power struggle involved covert partnerships. It mattered who your allies were more than just the kingdom you controlled. In the shadows, monarchs built a network of ties that could help tip the scales in their favor when needed.

The art of diplomatic posturing emerged. Think of this like a large chessboard where every move is a well-thought-out diplomatic. Using strategic projections of power and fragility, monarchs shaped the opinions of allies and neighboring kingdoms.

Let's now extend the viewpoint. This historical voyage investigates the elusive factors that molded people's destinies rather than a simple retelling of past occurrences. The shadows of the past emerge as we flip the pages, beckoning us to unravel the complexities of silent influence. It's an introduction to the manipulative sciences, with more in the upcoming chapters.

Welcome to this historical tour of manipulation, where every age contributes a new layer to the canvas of silent dominance. The rich painting of human history is further enhanced by the vivid strokes of the medieval courts and their dance of deception.

THE EARLIEST INSTANCES OF QUIET DOMINANCE STRATEGIES.

Let us continue our historical exploration, but this time, we will return to the early days of subduing opposition. It's similar to the pivotal point at which centuries of refinement transform manipulation into art. Join me as we explore the mysteries sewn into the fabric of power that have shaped civilizations' fates as we travel through time together.

1. Mesoamerican Interests:

Imagine the birthplace of civilization, Mesopotamia, as the historic playground where covert plotting evolved into a form of diplomacy. Leaders in this enormous land were more than just rulers; they were expert navigators of the complex city-states of Babylon and Ur.

Let's explore these city-states now. Think of them as separate kingdoms, with opportunities and problems unique to each. The rulers of Babylon and Ur were not satisfied to merely rule their towns; they desired to control the entire political system. As a result, they formed partnerships and strategic alliances with other city-states to fortify their positions and obtain an advantage.

Informal talks resembled the backroom dealings in a major political chess match. Not only did leaders make choices in public, but they also had private conversations and struck arrangements that would determine the future of their city-states. The key to power lay in a realm of whispers and subliminal gestures.

Let us now discuss the first murmurs of silent supremacy. This was about developing the art of persuasion rather than just using force to rule. Mesopotamian leaders laid the groundwork for deceitful behaviors that would reverberate throughout history, much like architects.

Think of this as the vast drama of political maneuvering's opening act. With its quiet cunning, Mesopotamia created the conditions for the complex power dance that would take place over decades and civilizations. The lasting influence of Mesopotamian diplomacy is demonstrated by the echoes of these antiquated intrigues that may still be heard today.

2. The Mystery of Egypt's Temples:

Imagine yourself in the opulent surrounds of an Egyptian temple and seeing a mystery event take place. Priests and scribes, keepers of particular information, had a distinct function within these magnificent buildings. They were not your typical characters; they were like secret guardians, using deeply symbolic rituals and symbols to orchestrate covert control.

Let us examine these symbols and rituals. They communicated significant ideas and values like a secret language; they weren't merely for show. The scribes and priests were skilled in gently influencing people's thoughts and beliefs through this language. It was about weaving an unseen effect through the fundamental fabric of spiritual activities, not about using force.

Consider the temples as more than just skyscrapers. They were havens for manipulation of beliefs as well as places of worship. Priests and scribes took advantage of the fact that people visited these locations in search of spiritual advice to sway their opinions gently.

This impact extended beyond a particular period, serving as a model for subdued domination tactics in many contexts. The mystical force that Egyptian temples possessed created a foundation for a type of influence that cut beyond historical boundaries and profoundly impacted how spirituality and beliefs were combined.

3. Greek Philosophers and Orators:

Imagine yourself in the bustling ancient Greek marketplace, where an amazing thing occurs. The Sophists and philosophers were working hard in this lively agora, like expert artisans, to transform the technique of persuasion into a potent weapon. However, precisely what were Sophists? Consider them skilled orators who could persuade listeners with their words and philosophers as profound thinkers who ponder life's important issues. Let us now discuss spoken language. It evolved into a type of silent force and stopped talking only for the sake of talking. These influences shaped people's opinions and worldviews by using the power of persuasion rather than weapons like swords or shields.

Imagine the agoras of Corinth and Athens as periods when this silent force operated. The philosophers and Sophists were not merely engaging in friendly banter; they were performing on a stage, enticing the audience with their persuasiveness and eloquence. It resembled a magic show in that words could change people's thoughts and perceptions. Let's add a little more information now. The agoras were centers of ideas as well as marketplaces for commerce. In addition to buying and selling, people congregated for discussions and disputes. It was a vibrant place where divergent viewpoints and persuasive techniques danced together engagingly.

Thus, the groundwork for subdued domination was being established in these agoras. The Sophists and philosophers' persuasiveness and eloquence heralded the birth of a subtle power that would reverberate through the ages, influencing the dissemination of ideas and the formation of opinions.

4. Unity and Power in Classical China:

Imagine entering the serene courts of ancient China, where an extraordinary event occurred. It was like witnessing a beautiful ballet, not just rulers shouting commands. The individuals surrounding the monarchs, known as courtiers and emperors, performed a silent ballet in which deeds spoke louder than words.

Let's concentrate on this dance now. It was a quiet ballet performed by gestures rather than a joyful performance with music and twirls. A short gesture like a nod or a slight movement could say more than a long discourse. They communicated in the great arena of imperial power using a silent language.

Speaking of symbolic gifts, let's. They were more than just gifts; they were like very symbolic messages. Every gift had a function: forge connections, demonstrate loyalty, or issue a subtle warning. Without saying a word, the strategic game of symbol trading communicated a lot. Then came the subdued threats.

Think of this as a game of chess when threats are implied rather than outright stated. Like a calculated play on the imperial chessboard, it hinted at implications without saying them out loud.

Let's zoom out a little now. These quiet tactics created a complex fabric rather than being separate incidents. It is like weaving swaying threads across the imperial power corridors. This was more than just governance; this was a political art that combined the elegant movements of a political ballet with the tranquil idea of harmony. The subtle methods of control employed by Chinese dynasties have left a lasting impression, generating a legacy that continues to influence our comprehension of power relations.

5. The Strategic Alliances of the Roman Senate:

As you enter the revered chambers of the Roman Senate, a narrative begins to take shape. It's more than just a venue for conversations—it's where the mundane operations of authority take on tremendous significance. Senators were masters of political manipulation, much like competent players in a strategy game.

Now, let's talk about strategic alliances. Consider the Senate a chessboard with senators acting as pieces moving to improve their places. These well-thought-out alliances were created to secure power and influence; they were not hasty judgments.

Let's now discuss loyalty. Senators demonstrated their loyalty as a subdued weapon rather than merely discussing it. Imagine this as a dance, where each step is carefully considered to demonstrate allegiance strategically. Inside the Senate, it was a silent power play of sorts.

Consider the Roman Republic's mastery of silence on a vast scale. It was more important to consider who made the best decisions than who could shout the loudest. Every choice the senators made shaped the course of the Republic, much like a step in a complicated political ballet.

The Roman Republic's echoes demonstrate early mastery of quiet power and politics. It was about taking calculated risks as much as it was about creating noise. Every calculated move in this political ballet made a lasting impression on history, demonstrating the skill of covert maneuvers that shaped ancient Rome's politics.

6. Medieval Courts: Deceitful Courts:

Imagine traveling back to medieval Europe, when the courts served as deceitful and ceremonial spaces. Like expert strategists, nobility and kings developed the art of deceit into a well-honed skill. It was more than just dressing up and perching on thrones; it was about engaging in a game in which each movement had a specific meaning.

Let's now discuss coded language. It was a method of conversing with subliminal implications, not a secret code as in a spy film. Monarchs and nobility had a way of speaking that outsiders might not fully comprehend. It resembled a discreet conversation in full view, with only those privy to the true meaning.

A key element of this medieval chess match was the formation of covert alliances. The nobility was not just thinking about their realms but also cultivating relationships behind the scenes. Imagine this as a network of trust and shared interests that reach into hidden chambers where kingdoms' outcomes were decided in whispers, far beyond the great halls.

And then there came deft diplomacy. Not only were ambassadors sent and treaties signed, but a deliberate ballet of words and gestures portrayed strength or frailty. The courts evolved into a political theater where each action was a performance meant to sway public opinion.

Let's zoom out a little now. This deceptive dance wasn't just a game; it signaled the beginning of a time when using silent influence to gain power required sophisticated tools. Not only were castles and courts magnificent buildings, but they also served as stages for elaborate dramas in which aristocrats and kings demonstrated their skill at deceit—this historical period profoundly affected how politics and power were fought for generations to come.

Every ancient culture we study contributes a different chapter to the unfolding tale of manipulation as we go further into the chapters that lead to a world of covert dominating tactics. These historical incidents are more than just narratives; they serve as the foundation for the manipulative techniques we currently research. Join us as we turn the pages and glimpse the complex dance of influence that will be revealed in the next chapters of this interpretation of human conduct.

CHAPTER 3
The Interpretation Of Human Conduct

Imagine standing at the crossroads of minds, where every glance and word is a clue to the mystery of human behavior. This Chapter beckons us into the fascinating realm of "The Interpretation of Human Conduct," where motives remain hidden, and gestures speak their own language. The curtain of mystery is drawn aside as we enter this Chapter, exposing the complexities of interpreting the silent symphony of the human psyche. Get ready to go on a journey that challenges perceptions and reveals the actual artistry of interpretation. This voyage pushes us to examine the minute details woven throughout human behavior.

THE PSYCHOLOGICAL BASIS OF HUMAN CONDUCT.

We begin our investigation into the nature of human behavior by exploring the deep levels of the psychological underpinnings that determine our behavior in such a complicated way. The complexity of this psychological underpinning is revealed by the following points, which offer a sophisticated view of the motivations, feelings, thought processes, social dynamics, and individual variations that together form the complex fabric of human behavior.

1. Experiencing Silent Orchestrations: A Journey into the Depths of the Unconscious Mind.

The unconscious mind is a mysterious realm of mental processes where ideas and emotions function without conscious awareness.

Let's investigate this secret world where desires, anxieties, and motivations influence our behavior covertly and without our knowledge.

Imagine the unconscious mind as a hidden vault full of memories and thoughts we aren't completely aware of in our regular thoughts. It shapes our behavior in ways we may not be mindful of, acting as the behavior's behind-the-scenes director. We must study this deeper layer by dissecting the layers of our conscious knowledge. It's similar to discovering unseen factors influencing our choices and how we relate to others.

Let's now discuss hidden agendas. The unconscious mind conceals intentions beneath the surface, such as hidden motivations behind our actions. These motivations, which stem from innate tendencies, past encounters, or unsaid feelings, subtly impact our decisions. It's similar to having an unseen guide lead us along avenues we might not intentionally chose.

Subtle desires also exist in the background. Investigating the unconscious exposes a cache of desires and dreams that direct our behavior. Our conduct becomes more complex due to these desires occasionally conflicting with our conscious desires. It's similar to understanding mental whispers and cracking a code.

Thus, the unconscious mind is this enigmatic realm where much of what motivates us remains hidden. It's similar to a backstage area impacting the front of the show. Comprehending it aids in disentangling the intricacies behind our actions. Some of the things the unconscious mind can do on its own without assistance are as follows:

a. Fears that Lurk: Our innermost worries, such as phobias, anxieties, and unsolved traumas, are concealed within our minds in addition to thoughts and memories. These anxieties have the effect of shadows, influencing our perceptions and actions in day-to-day living. We need to explore these concerns, discover their origins, and assess the extent to which they influence our behavior to gain a deeper understanding of the inner workings of our brains.

Consider being afraid of heights or spiders. It's not just about being afraid in the heat of the moment; it's about how that anxiety might change how you deal with circumstances. For instance, you could avoid high locations like roller coasters and towering skyscrapers if you're afraid of heights. Although you may not always be aware of it, this dread is subtly influencing your decisions.

Let's now discuss fears. These may resemble anxieties that surface unseen to us. Giving a speech in front of an audience makes you queasy. You may not be completely conscious of this anxiety, yet it can nevertheless affect the choices you make. For example, you may avoid circumstances in which you must speak in front of a group.

Unresolved traumas are another issue. These are difficult or painful prior experiences that can still be present in our memories. For example, your current feelings toward dogs may be influenced by a negative childhood experience you had with them. That experience can influence your behavior, even if you're unaware of it. Thus, when we discuss the unconscious mind, we also discuss where our worries congregate. It's like a dimly lit chamber with shadowy corners, and we may illuminate these anxieties and how they affect our lives by investigating and comprehending them.

b. Tacit coordinator of behavior: Imagine the unconscious mind as a master conductor who works behind the scenes to arrange the symphony of human behavior expertly. Without conscious knowledge, it's like a maestro evaluating our surroundings, managing our emotions, and formulating our answers. Examining this covert orchestration uncovers the inner mechanisms that influence our behavior and the nuanced ways our unconscious mind directs us.

Let's now discuss why delving into the unconscious mind is akin to a profound voyage of self-discovery. It's important to be open to comprehending the complexity within each of us rather than merely focusing on the obvious. Imagine this journey as casting a light into the recesses of our minds, where we face the desires, motivations, and anxieties that, frequently from the shadows, affect our behavior.

Let's dissect it using a concrete example. Consider an instance where you experienced a gut instinct, such as when you met someone for the first time. Without conscious awareness, your unconscious mind digests small information and creates impressions. By examining the unconscious, one can get insights beyond what is immediately apparent and effectively pull back the curtain on these processes.

Consider your motivations and desires now. Though they aren't always on our minds, they significantly impact our behavior. Consider someone who appears to be constantly looking for approval. Although they may not be aware of it, this need influences their decisions as they seek approval and recognition.

The process of deciphering the unconscious is akin to piecing together a puzzle. Every item we uncover deepens our comprehension of the motivations behind our actions. This voyage helps us understand the subtle forces that permeate our behavior and go beyond what we know.

c. Motivation as the Driving Force: Exposing the Complex Nature of Human Behavior. Motivation is like the fuel that keeps us running in the complicated realm of human behavior, influencing our lives. As we dive deeper into Motivation, let's examine the factors influencing our decision Motivations.

Fundamentally, Motivation functions as a road map directing our actions and decisions. The forces that drive us to act and make decisions combine internal and external factors. Understanding the breadth and complexity of the motivations forming the intricate web influencing our behavior is essential to understanding why we act in the ways we do truly.

Let's now discuss the motivational force behind Motivation. It covers a wide range, from basic survival instincts to the more nuanced desires that make us human. First up is the urge for survival. This is like a super ancient force hardwired into our bodies, pushing us to find food, shelter, and safety. It's the root of many of our basic behaviors.

Beyond just survival, there's the pursuit of pleasure. Our human experience is directly tied to the desire for joy, happiness, and fulfillment. Whether it's finding pleasure in experiences, relationships, or personal achievements, this desire influences the stories of our lives, pushing us to do things that bring happiness and contentment.

Then, there's the quest for social validation. This powerful motivator guides our behavior to fit in and be recognized by others. The desire for approval, belonging, and acknowledgment often shapes how we interact with people. We navigate societal expectations and relationships, trying to match accepted standards and gain validation from others.

Understanding these different motivations helps us see why individuals act a certain way and show how many influences create the big picture of people's behavior. It's like a tapestry where every thread represents a motivational force pushing us forward. As we deal with survival instincts, seek pleasure, and aim for social validation, Motivation becomes a central theme in the story of being human.

In summary, looking into Motivation as the force driving human behavior lets us examine the complicated mechanisms behind our decisions and actions. It's a journey that uncovers the layers of complexity in our motivational landscape, giving us deep insights into the various reasons that shape the intricate story of our lives.

2. Emotions as Silent Messengers: Illuminating the Profound Influence on Human Conduct.

Emotions become important signals in understanding why people act as they do. They silently convey much about what's happening inside us, guiding our reactions and shaping how we see things. This essay digs into the world of emotions, decoding their unspoken language – from quick facial expressions to our bodies' subtle moves. Through this exploration, we learn about emotions' powerful influence on the intricate dance of how people behave.

Emotions are like messengers, quietly telling us what's happening inside us. They're the feelings that respond to our thoughts, experiences, and interactions – ranging from happiness and sadness to anger and fear. Emotions speak eloquently beyond words, often revealing more than what we say.

Let's talk about micro-expressions, those tiny and quick facial expressions that happen in a flash. They give us a peek into someone's emotional world, showing authentic feelings before they get controlled consciously. Understanding these quick expressions needs a sharp awareness, letting us catch the genuine emotions that might be under the surface.

Then there's body language – the silent way our bodies express emotions through gestures, postures, and movements. How we stand, move, and use gestures contribute to this silent language of emotions. Unraveling this complex tapestry helps us interpret the unspoken messages conveyed through body language, giving us more insight into how people behave.

Looking at emotions as messengers goes beyond just individuals. In the intricate dance of how people act, group dynamics are influenced by the shared emotional states of individuals in a given situation. Emotions become a collective force, shaping the mood of a place, affecting decision-making, and contributing to the overall vibe of social interactions.

Understanding the silent language of emotions is a subtle skill. It involves having emotional intelligence – being aware of your feelings and understanding others feel. As we navigate the complex world of how people act, this emotional intelligence becomes a useful guide, helping us better understand relationships and social situations.

To sum it up, emotions, as these silent messengers, are a big part of how people behave. Exploring micro-expressions, body language, and the collective impact of emotions reveals the complex dynamics underlying our interactions. It encourages us to pay attention to the quiet language spoken by our emotions, leading to a deeper understanding of ourselves and others in the intricate dance of human behavior.

3. Cognitive Processes and Decision-Making: Unveiling the Intricacies Shaping Human Conduct.

In understanding how people act, think of the mind as a silent architect. It's like the behind-the-scenes worker processing information, figuring out situations, and helping make decisions. This essay dives into cognitive processes like seeing and understanding things, remembering stuff, and solving problems. By learning how these cognitive intricacies work, we learn about the mechanisms that shape how people interpret and deal with their experiences.

Let's start with perception – how we make sense of the world around us. It's like a dance between our senses and what's happening outside us. From the colors we see to the sounds we hear, perception is the lens through which we create our version of reality. Understanding how perception works shows us how people pay attention to things, sift through information, and build their picture of what's real.

Next up is memory, like a big storage space for our past experiences and what we've learned. Memory is the canvas where our history gets painted as we go through life. It affects how we see current situations, make choices, and respond based on previous events. Figuring out how memory works shows us the complicated link between remembering things and forming the way we behave.

Then there's problem-solving, which kicks in when we face challenges. It's all about finding solutions to problems or puzzles. This cognitive process is key to how people navigate their experiences. Looking at how people solve problems shows us how they approach issues – using logic or creative thinking. This is where the mind becomes an active player in steering people's behavior.

All these cognitive intricacies together create the background for how people act. It's like an unseen conductor leading a symphony, influencing how individuals understand information, remember past stuff, and tackle problems. The mix of these cognitive processes adds layers to how people go through their experiences, making human behavior rich and diverse.

Understanding these cognitive intricacies is crucial in figuring out how people behave. It gives us insights into how they process information, make choices, and see the world around them. As we navigate this cognitive landscape, we see how complex it is, realizing that human behavior isn't just about what happens outside us but is also shaped by what goes on in the depths of the mind.

To summarize, digging into cognitive processes and decision-making shows us the complex machinery behind human behavior. From perception to memory and problem-solving, each part of our thinking contributes to how we act, shaping how we understand and respond to the world. This understanding gives us a deep look into the silent forces working within the cognitive realm, which sets the stage for the story of human behavior.

4. Social Dynamics and Behavioral Influences: Crafting the Tapestry of Human Conduct.

In understanding how people act, think of it like a big woven fabric, and the threads that make it up are the social dynamics. This essay examines how these social dynamics influence our interactions and decisions. It checks out how things like cultural norms, what society expects, and our relationships with others impact how we behave. In psychology, we explore these social dynamics and see how they act like silent architects, shaping behavior in the bigger picture of how we interact.

Humans have been social beings from the time they entered the world. Social dynamics start with following cultural norms – like unwritten rules about how to behave, manners, and what society expects. These norms, often learned from childhood, make a structure that shapes how individuals behave within the big picture of a particular culture. In our exploration of psychology, we see how sticking to these norms becomes a guiding force, paving the way for societal expectations to become a big deal.

Societal expectations are a strong force in social dynamics. They set up norms and standards that people are pushed to meet. It could be things like what education you should get, career choices, or the roles you play in your family. These expectations silently shape behavior based on what's considered successful and acceptable. As we dive into societal expectations, we discover the subtle pushes and restrictions people face, impacting their choices and actions in line with what's seen as normal.

Then there are our close relationships, like family, friends, and romantic partners. These relationships add personal touches to the big fabric of social dynamics. Influences from these relationships act like whispers, guiding behavior through emotional ties, shared experiences, and the give-and-take that comes with social bonds. Studying social dynamics involves how these relationships become powerful influencers, shaping individual behavior and adding to the complex web of how society interacts.

Social dynamics don't just stay in individual relationships; they also stretch to groups in larger communities. People deal with social hierarchies, power structures, and shared identities in groups. Understanding the psychological side of things shows us the subtle ways group dynamics affect behavior, creating a sense of belonging, loyalty, and a shared purpose. The silent architects in group dynamics help shape behavior individually and as part of the whole group.

Looking at social dynamics in psychology is like exploring the forces that shape how people behave in the big dance of society. It makes us see that behavior isn't just about what individuals decide; it's closely tied to the expectations, norms, and relationships that make up the social fabric. As we move through the complexities of how people interact, understanding these silent architects of social dynamics gives us deep insights into the motivations and influences guiding behavior in the larger context of society.

To sum it up, digging into social dynamics and what influences behavior shows us the intricate forces that create the fabric of human conduct. Cultural norms, societal expectations, and personal relationships act like silent architects, molding behavior and adding to the lively interaction within the big mosaic of society. This understanding helps us appreciate the complexity of human behavior, recognizing that the whispers of social dynamics play a crucial role in the unfolding story of how we all interact.

5. Individual Differences and Personality: The Unique Palette of Human Conduct.

In looking at how people act, we're diving into the psychology behind it, especially regarding what makes each person different and their personality traits. This essay explores the unique qualities that shape human personality – temperament, character, and personal history. Each person is like an artist using a special palette, adding colors to the big picture of human interaction. This part breaks down how these individual differences and personality traits shape and influence behavior, bringing out the special shades that color the canvas of how people interact.

First, we've got to acknowledge the huge range of individual differences that make one person different. These differences cover many things, from how people think and feel to what they like socially and what they think is right or wrong. Temperament, the natural set of characteristics influencing how someone reacts to things, is a big part of understanding these differences. Some folks might naturally lean towards being outgoing and enjoying social stuff (extraversion), while others might prefer being alone and thinking (introversion). These differences are key to figuring out how people express themselves in the human landscape.

Then there's a character, another important piece of individual differences. It's about the learned parts of a person's personality, shaped by experiences, values, and what they believe is right. This part shows a person's ability for empathy (understanding others), integrity (doing what's right), and resilience (bouncing back from tough times). Understanding character helps see how people handle moral questions, make ethical choices, and do things that benefit everyone.

Personal history is the third part of the personality mosaic. Each person brings a unique story of life experiences, cultural influences, and important moments. Personal history is like a collection of memories shaping how someone sees and reacts to the world. Exploring personal history shows layers of resilience, vulnerability, and adaptability that affect how people handle challenges, build relationships, and deal with the complexities of human interaction.

Looking into individual differences and personality traits is about celebrating the diversity in the human experience. It's a reminder to appreciate the special qualities everyone adds to the big picture of society. Like no two brushstrokes on a canvas are the same, no two people have the same temperament, character, or personal history. Understanding this diversity helps us appreciate the depth and richness of human behavior.

More than just understanding, recognizing individual differences and personality traits has practical uses in everyday life – in education, workplaces, relationships, and how societies are structured. Adjusting our approaches, how we talk, and the help we offer based on understanding these differences makes these interactions more effective. With its unique patterns and combinations, the human personality mosaic becomes a source of strength and resilience in the bigger picture of human society.

In wrapping things up, exploring individual differences and personality in the psychological aspect shows the unique colors each person adds to how people behave. Temperament, character, and personal history blend to create a mosaic reflecting the diversity and complexity of being human. Embracing this diversity helps us understand behavior better and sets the stage for building inclusive and compassionate societies that celebrate the unique qualities in the grand masterpiece of human interaction.

As we continue our journey through the psychological landscape, these ideas act like guides, helping us navigate the intricate terrain of understanding. The mind is both the artist and the canvas, contributing to the grand composition of human behavior. In the next paragraphs, we'll dive even deeper, unraveling specific aspects of the psychological basis and gaining a more profound understanding of the silent forces at play in interpreting human conduct.

CAUSES AND MOTIVATORS OF HUMAN CONDUCT.

As we delve deeper into the psychological basis, the focus now shifts to the intricate interplay of causes and motivators underlying human conduct. Understanding the roots of behavior and the driving forces that propel individuals forward is crucial in unraveling the complexities of the silent orchestrations within the psyche.

1. Unraveling Causes:

When it comes to why we do what we do, it's like digging into the soil of our actions and uncovering a network of roots. These roots, or causes, are various and can be traced back to a mix of things happening around us and within our thinking.

Consider external factors as triggers, like a switch that ignites a behavior. For example, assume you observe someone shivering in the cold. This external stimulus drives you to lend them a jacket, illustrating the cause-and-effect relationship between the environment and your humanitarian action.

On the flip side, internal psychological processes are like the unseen gears turning within our minds. Picture someone feeling uncomfortable before a large presentation — the internal reason for nervous thoughts and feelings directly affects their conduct, potentially making them more cautious or expressive throughout the presentation.

Delving into these factors is like untangling a tangled web. It allows us to recognize the strings linking different elements of our lives and behaviors. Understanding these triggers gives us insights into the deep reasons that steer us. Causes become like jigsaw pieces; when we fit them together, we provide a fuller picture of why people follow down various life pathways. Some causes to study include external stimuli, environmental conditions, and the fascinating interaction of internal psychological processes.

2. The Motivational Landscape:

Motivation isn't just a simple "push" to accomplish anything; it's a complicated environment, much like a beautiful garden with numerous flowers. Imagine intrinsic motivators as the blooms anchored in their beliefs and objectives like the robust sunflower rising tall in the garden. On the other hand, extrinsic motivators, such as prizes and social acceptability, act like the rain and sunlight that nurture and assist these flowers blossom.

In our daily lives, this motivating garden influences every decision we make. For instance, a student studying late into the night can be driven by the intrinsic desire for knowledge or the extrinsic objective of getting good grades. Similarly, a person putting in extra effort at work could be driven by the inherent worth of accomplishment or the extrinsic reward of a promotion.

Exploring this garden illustrates the intricate web of desires, needs, and goals that fuel our behavior. It's like reading a treasure map where each incentive is a clue leading to the next stage in our trip. As we navigate this broad array of incentives, we acquire crucial insights into what genuinely moves us, giving a vivid picture of the interesting interplay between our motives and behaviors. In the paragraphs below, we'll cover many types of motivators.

a. Exploring Intrinsic Motivations:

When it comes to what fires our internal fire, we're talking about intrinsic motivators – those deep-down reasons that make us do things because we want to. Think of it as your cheerleader, cheering you on from within.

Personal values are like the compass guiding your decisions. If honesty, for example, is one of your basic values, you may find yourself speaking up even in difficult situations because integrity is your internal compass. Your engine runs on gasoline, which is your passion. The natural desire to make art becomes a motivating factor if you enjoy painting. You paint because art makes you happy and fulfilled, not to win praise from others.

A mission in life is similar to having a feeling of purpose. Being the greatest parent you can be or positively influencing your community could suffice. Your daily activities are shaped and given purpose by this innate drive. Consider a student who selects a degree based on their passion for the subject rather than because it would lead to a well-paying career. Here, intrinsic motivators direct their academic path and impact decisions consistent with their true identity.

Deciphering the hidden language of our motives is similar to realizing how our personal beliefs, interests, and sense of purpose influence our behavior. It gives more context to why we act as we do by revealing the real, self-driven reasons that influence our behavior.

b. Motivation from without:

Let us now discuss extrinsic motivators, external cues that prompt us to behave in a particular manner. It feels like our environment is a stage, and the outside factors are the directors controlling how we act. Like unseen scripts, societal expectations define what is deemed appropriate or normal. Consider a person who selects a profession based on social expectations or respect rather than passion. In this case, their actions are shaped by the outside pressures of society's expectations.

Another participant in this game of external incentive is peer pressure. Consider it a subliminal murmur that begs for compliance. Teenagers, for example, may begin dressing a specific way or forming certain habits to blend in with their friends, illustrating how outside factors can affect individual decisions. Rewards and praise from outside sources serve as dangling carrots that entice people to engage in particular actions. Imagine a worker who puts in a lot of effort to get promoted; in this case, the prospect of a reward serves as an external motivator, spurring the worker's commitment and hard work.

Investigating extrinsic motivators is akin to unlocking the code that shapes our behavior without our knowledge. It's realizing how peer pressure, societal norms, and outside incentives play in the behavior dance. It draws attention to the fine line between the outside world's impact and our personal decisions, highlighting how our actions are intertwined with the environment.

C. Implicit Influences:

Let's now explore the fascinating world of unconscious influences, which operate behind the scenes in our thoughts to affect our behavior without us even being aware. Think of them as the backstage staff of our minds.

Unconscious biases are similar to our brains' autopilot mode. Imagine, for example, meeting someone new and, for reasons you can't quite put your finger on, instantly connecting with them or feeling uneasy. These prejudices, frequently formed by cultural standards or prior encounters, subtly direct our actions.

Anxieties that linger in the background of our thoughts also contribute. Consider a person who shies away from public speaking due to a past humiliation. Their decisions are subtly influenced by the dread, which is based on an unresolved experience and directs them away from anxious circumstances.

Past events that aren't quite resolved haunt us like ghosts, always present in the background of our thoughts. If a person had a bad experience with an authority figure when they were younger, their attitude toward them as this unresolved event may unintentionally influence adults.

Investigating these unintentional influences is similar to turning on a light in a poorly lighted space. It makes visible the minute influences that mold our actions behind our conscious minds. The story of human behavior becomes more complex due to our increased awareness of these underlying forces, which help us comprehend why humans behave in particular ways. It's similar to solving a riddle where the answers are hidden in the corners of our brains and influence our behavior in ways we might not be aware of.

THE INTERACTION BETWEEN MOTIVATORS AND CAUSES.

Explore the complicated relationship between causes and motivators, which, when combined, provide a mesmerizing symphony that reflects the complexity of human behavior. In this section, we look at how causes function as sparks that ignite the flames of motivators and how motivators, on the other hand, enhance the influence of causes. Imagine it as a dance floor, where the harmonious interaction of these two components choreographs every person's move.

Causes initiate action by acting as catalysts. Think of a cause as the first domino to fall, starting a domino effect. For example, the resilience motivation may be triggered by a difficult life event. When faced with hardship, the person finds courage, demonstrating how causes pave the way for motivators to appear.

In turn, motivators increase the influence of causes. Consider them to be the wind beneath behavior's wings. If the seed is the cause, then the growing soil and sunlight are the motivators. For instance, an individual who is passionate about environmental conservation could use their intrinsic incentive to fuel their drive to make positive changes in response to a personal loss.

Unraveling a compelling narrative is akin to traveling via the investigation of causes and motivators. Every motive is a protagonist guiding the story, and every cause is a plot element. These intertwined strands weave a tapestry of stories just waiting to be told by human conduct.

This investigation is more than behavior analysis; it's about understanding the intricate mental orchestrations. Motivators and causes work together like expert musicians in a symphony to create the beautiful melody of human behavior. Through this trip, we discover the depth and richness of the silent orchestrations and realize that the interplay of causes and motivators creates a deep and vivid picture of our motivations. Stay with me as we unfold a new chapter on techniques of silence domination.

CHAPTER 4
Techniques Of Silence Domination

We enter Chapter 4: Techniques of Silent Domination, which takes us into the enigmatic realm of human psychology, where invisible forces subtly shape our beliefs and actions. Imagine a world in which silent domination masters use strategies that leave a lasting impression on the minds of onlookers and influence works its magic in the background, transforming the art of persuasion into a captivating dance. As we turn the pages of this chapter, get ready for an in-depth look at fascinating techniques that go beyond the obvious, beckoning you to investigate the best-kept secrets that control silent dominance in the intricate realm of human behavior.

Imagine this chapter as an expedition into the hidden passageways of the psyche, where the influence puppeteers deftly manipulate minute details. These methods leave a lasting impression on our thoughts and deeds, much like secret weapons that are subtle yet effective. It's like figuring out an old map showing you the clever maneuvers of people who can dance with persuasion.

We come across methods that function in the world of the invisible as we read through these pages. Imagine a situation in which well-placed phrases, mirroring, and subtle clues all function as instruments in this quiet orchestra of influence. For example, someone skilled in these methods could silently duplicate your body language with subtle body language, building rapport and trust without saying anything.

Get ready for an exciting voyage through this chapter as psychological tricks are revealed like in a suspenseful movie.

Every tactic, from the deft application of social proof to the skillful construction of narratives, is a paintbrush on the canvas of human behavior. Understanding these tactics is not enough; you also need to spot the complex dance between those who control and those who are manipulated, providing an intriguing window into the world of silent dominance.

THE ART OF INFLUENCE.

Our next stop is a deep dive into the practice of influence art as we continue to travel across the terrain of quiet dominance. This trip is like navigating the subtle currents that shape human behavior; it reveals how deftly manipulating our ideas and actions may shape them.

The ensuing paragraphs take us on a thorough exploration of the subtleties of influence, an elusive power that functions in the background. Think of it like a delicate ballet in which manipulation takes on a devious disguise, and persuasion becomes an enthralling art form. Understanding the subtle dynamics that influence people's decisions without them even recognizing it is more important than using force or coercion.

Think about social proof, which other people's actions can significantly impact. Imagine yourself checking out a brand-new eatery that is crowded with patrons. The busy atmosphere makes you feel as though this establishment must be fantastic, making you decide to try it. It's a soft current of influence that subtly directs your decision based on the behaviors of others in your immediate vicinity.

As we delve deeper into influence, we come across strategies like framing, in which information is presented in a way that gently alters perception. Consider getting a discount presented as "Save $10" instead of "10% Off." This change in perspective will affect how you assess the offer. It's a complex ballet between words and context that illustrates the nuances of influencing art.

This chapter flows like a road map, linking the study of quiet dominance to the sophisticated strategies employed by people skilled in persuasion. It's about figuring out the tiny currents of persuasion that run through our everyday lives and realizing how powerful they influence our decisions and behavior. So fasten your seatbelts and join us as we embark on a journey to explore the realm where the mastery of influence comes to life, showcasing the intriguing interaction between human behavior and the creative methods that mold it.

1. Unspoken Communication: The unspoken language that subtly molds our encounters is vital to the interesting realm of influence. Body language, facial gestures, and other subtle indicators that apply subtle brushstrokes to the influence canvas are like having a hidden code that transcends words.

Consider body language as an example. During a conversation, picture someone listening intently, keeping eye contact, and nodding in accord. These nonverbal cues give the spoken words more substance by expressing interest, comprehension, and agreement. Conversely, averted eyes or crossed arms might convey unease or disagreement, which adds a subtle undertone that affects the exchange.

Another level of this nonverbal communication is expressed through facial expressions. A sincere grin can foster a friendly, trusting environment that increases people's openness to your influence. On the other hand, a furrowed brow or raised eyebrow might convey doubt or bewilderment, offering a subtly challenging look to the power in action.

Nonverbal cues are comparable to impact language's punctuation. Subtle indications such as a brief pause before a point is important or a deliberate hand motion highlighting important concepts can enhance the impact of spoken words. Imagine a professional speaker highlighting key points with precise gestures to increase the impact and memorability of their message.

Comprehending this nonverbal communication reveals the authority possessed by individuals skilled in persuasion. It's similar to possessing a secret advantage, in which a quick gesture or nod can say more than a long speech. Understanding the creative dance of persuasion requires mastery of the silent language, which may be gained through examining unspoken communication. This allows us to obtain insights into the subtle orchestration of influence.

2. Psychological Triggers: Recognizing the nuanced cues that appeal to the human psyche is a competence in the field of influence. It's similar to having a playbook that can influence feelings, wants, and how people make decisions. This trip explores the world of psychological triggers—those unseen switches that, when activated, can elicit strong reactions and influence choices.

Let's dissect it. Consider the idea of framing, which states that perception is shaped by how information is presented. Think about a product labeled as "90% fat-free" instead of "10% fat." The framing of one product plays on the good aspect of being fat-free, while the other plays on the negative aspect of being 10% fat, which may cause you to consider it a healthier option.

Another psychological factor at work is priming. Consider it as preparing the groundwork for a specific way of thinking. Before making a purchase, for instance, you are likely to link a luxury good with exclusivity and richness if you are given photographs of the item. This could persuade you to choose a more expensive option.

Cognitive biases are analogous to the mental shortcuts we employ during information processing. For example, the anchoring bias happens when we emphasize the first piece of information we come across. Consider a negotiation when the first offer is made; that offer serves as an anchor, affecting offers and decisions made later.

Knowing these triggers is similar to knowing the moves in a chess game regarding the art of influence. Expert influencers use framing to highlight specifics, condition others to think a certain way, and use cognitive biases to influence choices. It's an exact dance, with each step planned to elicit a particular reaction.

The goal of studying the landscape of psychological triggers is to identify the factors that inherently affect our mental processes rather than to manipulate them. Disclosing this influence technique illuminates the strategic dance in which triggers are skillfully used to arouse feelings, satisfy needs, and influence choices. It's like pulling back the curtain to see the complex machinery that motivates human behavior, demonstrating the intriguing interaction between psychology and skillful influencing techniques.

3. Adaptive Influence: Flexibility is like having a secret weapon in the complex dance of influence. This section of our investigation explores the field of adaptive influence, in which adept influencers tailor their strategy to suit various personalities, circumstances, and settings. It's about realizing that no two situations are the same and that influencing art demands customization.

Let's say you're attempting to persuade two pals to go on a hike. You emphasize the fun and exhilaration of finishing a difficult trail because one of your friends is daring and enjoys difficulties. You draw attention to the quiet terrain and moments of tranquility during the hike for your other companion, who appreciates leisure and gorgeous surroundings. Here, adaptive persuasion entails customizing your argument to each friend's distinct tastes to maximize the possibility that they will be convinced to join based on what personally appeals to them.

Like chameleons, adaptive influencers effortlessly modify their tactics to suit the personalities they come across. For instance, when attempting to persuade a coworker, you should modify your communication style to fit their preferences. While some people are more receptive to emotional pleas, others may be better off with rational arguments. The skill is identifying these subtleties and adjusting your strategy to establish a more meaningful connection with them.

Contexts and circumstances are also important in adaptive persuasion. Imagine a salesperson presenting a product. In an official corporate context, they could emphasize how economical and efficient it is. On the other hand, in a more relaxed setting, they highlight the product's ease of use and lifestyle advantages. They raise their chances of striking a chord with their audience by customizing their pitch to the particular situation.

Understanding adaptive persuasion is about appreciating and acknowledging the range of responses people have, not about using manipulation. Influencers dance deftly through the dynamic terrain of human interactions, tailoring their routines to the particular beats of each circumstance and individual. This artwork reveals the capacity to relate to others on a real level and mentor them toward a goal in a way that is personalized, sincere, and considerate of their uniqueness.

4. Mastery of Storytelling: The power to captivate an audience through storytelling is comparable to having a magic wand in the world of influence. This segment of our voyage explores the fascinating field of master storytelling, wherein storytellers employ narratives as powerful instruments. It's about dissecting the craft of telling stories that influence viewpoints and grabbing readers' attention. Let's examine how narrative fits into the symphony of impact in more detail.

Consider yourself attempting to convince your coworkers to support a new initiative. Rather than deluging them with data, tell them a story about a successful project that resembles yours, emphasizing the difficulties encountered, the teamwork required, and the successful conclusion. Not only are you providing knowledge with this story, but you're also stimulating your team's imagination, appealing to their feelings, and gently nudging them toward a more optimistic outlook on the upcoming endeavor.

A skillfully written narrative draws the audience in and immerses them in a world of feelings and experiences, much like a fascinating adventure. Think of a brand that narrates its beginnings, challenges, and victories. Brands may establish a stronger connection with consumers and impact their purchasing decisions by creating a narrative around their journey.

Being a master of impact storytelling means knowing what makes a story gripping:

- A protagonist who can be identified with.
- A problem that needs to be solved.
- A satisfying conclusion.

Consider a motivational speaker who uses personal tales to enthuse their listeners. The speaker's message is made deeper by the relatable experiences that serve as a bridge to connect the speaker's message to the listeners' lives.

Creating a compelling story involves more than just using words; it also sows the seeds of influence. The narrative becomes a means of gently influencing choices and beliefs. Imagine a political leader presenting their vision through storytelling; the story becomes an effective instrument for influencing public opinion and winning over supporters.

As we discover the art of storytelling, it becomes clear that stories have a tremendous effect on our minds and are not merely for pleasure. Our worldview is shaped by stories, impacting our decisions and beliefs. Mastering storytelling with lasting impact involves crafting stories that captivate and leave a lasting impression on our choices and thoughts.

COVERT PERSUASION.

The focus now shifts to covert persuasion as we go farther into the quiet labyrinths of subtle dominance and manipulation. This is where influence works covertly, preventing people from realizing the puppet strings controlling their decisions. This section delves into the subtleties of covert persuasion, revealing the hidden strategies that mold behavior without being seen. They include the following:

1. Gentle Recommendations: It takes skill to sow the seeds of influence through subtly suggested ideas in persuasion. Consider it as planting microscopic seeds that become rooted in the mental soil. This section of our investigation delves into how influencers deftly insert recommendations into conversations and use well-chosen language, subliminal cues, and clever wording to steer choices without coercion. Let's explore the facets of this fascinating art form.

Imagine a situation when a friend needs to decide if they should sign up for a fitness class. Rather than telling the buddy, "You should join the class," an influencer can gently advise, "Imagine how great you'd feel after a few sessions." This way, the idea is planted gently, and the friend is helped to imagine a good outcome, increasing the likelihood that they would decide to join.

Similar to covert instructions concealed within a sentence are embedded commands. For example, the embedded command "picture" encourages you to imagine owning and utilizing the product, increasing the likelihood that you will purchase it. For example, a salesperson may say, "Picture yourself enjoying this product at home."

Strategic wording is the process of selecting words that elicit particular reactions. Imagine that a manager has a deadline that needs to be met by a team. The small change influences the team's approach to meeting the deadline in the phrase, which could be, "I'm confident you can complete this project efficiently," as opposed to, "I need you to finish this project quickly."

These imperceptible recommendations resemble soft prods toward the intended result. Expert influencers know the psychology of suggestion planting and see it's more about gently influencing people's thoughts than imposing their will. It resembles having a helpful guide point out noteworthy locations without forcing one to follow their path.

Understanding the delicate dance of influence is more important than manipulation as we delve into the art of subtle suggestion. It's admitting that the mind is open to these sown seeds, and the skill is in using them sensibly and morally. This section reveals the levels of this subtle art, in which influencers skillfully negotiate communication to subtly affect decisions without interfering with others' autonomy.

2. Anchoring in psychology: Anchoring is an interesting phenomenon in persuasion that can be used as a covert weapon in persuasive techniques. This method automatically links targeted stimuli and intended responses, which plays into human psychology. Explore the subtleties of psychological anchoring with me as we explore how influencers utilize clues, symbols, or gestures to direct others along preferred routes and elicit planned responses gradually.

Anchoring can be compared to mentally planting a flag. Imagine a situation when you come across a product that was once $100 but is now only $50—the first $100 is an anchor, affecting how you see the reduced amount. In light of the greater anchor, the $50 now seems like a terrific value, even though the product wasn't originally worth $100. Influencers do this by anchoring your perception, increasing the likelihood that you will see their product favorably.

Astute price strategists frequently employ anchoring in their plans. For example, a restaurant may place an expensive premium dish at the top of the menu. This is an anchor, making the other, marginally less costly dishes seem like sensible and alluring substitutes.

In time, anchoring is also effective. Imagine a salesperson informing you that a special offer will expire in two days. The deadline serves as an anchor, increasing the offer's perceived value and promoting a speedier decision-making process.

Anchors can also be gestures and symbols. Imagine introducing a presentation with a strong symbol used by the speaker. This sign into an anchor influences how you interpret the entire discussion. Similarly, a politician's signature gesture during an address might act as an anchor by connecting the gesture to specific feelings or concepts.

Psychological anchoring is about identifying the subtle ways our minds operate, not being duped. It's similar to realizing that familiar reference points are what our minds are trained to cling to. Anchoring is a strategic tool influencers use to generate these points of reference, leading us down mental routes that support their goals. Thus, in covert persuasion, we acquire insight into the unseen factors influencing our actions and perceptions as we peel back the layers of psychological anchoring.

3. Persuasion by Association: A potent force known as association is at work in covert persuasion. Influencers carefully associate themselves or their notions with admirable people, ideas, or positive imagery; it's almost like a magic trick. Let's examine how this operates in this section of the tour. Influencers, like expert puppeteers, subtly affect our thoughts and behaviors without us even recognizing them.

Consider association as creating buddies in your head. Envision a fresh brand linking itself to ecological sustainability. They establish a mental connection with you by associating the company with romantic ideas such as environmental sustainability. When you think about it, you may unintentionally identify the brand with good sentiments related to ecological stewardship.

Celebrities frequently turn into effective tools for associations. Imagine a well-known sports figure supporting a sports drink. Influencers establish a connection by associating the drink with a good perception of the athlete's athleticism and success. Perhaps you've thought, "If this athlete drinks it, maybe it's the secret to peak performance."

The association is a useful tool for politicians as well. Imagine a candidate displaying photos of disparate groups coming together as unifying symbols when they appear in public. They shape public opinion by deliberately placing themselves in front of positive visuals. Because of the subconscious link, people may equate the candidate with harmony and unity.

Association shapes stories in our thoughts, much like a silent storyteller. A tech corporation, for instance, can purposefully display its products alongside advancement and innovation. They shape your perception of their brand—connected to innovation and cutting-edge technology—by associating with positive ideas.

This idea deals with small mental shortcuts. Our thoughts see things more favorably when associated with good concepts or people. Influencers are masters of association; they carefully select favorable links to project a positive light on themselves or their concepts.

When we go into the nuances of association-based influence, the key is not to be susceptible to influence but to identify the unseen forces that mold our views. It's realizing how these minute relationships affect our opinions and actions, gently urging us to side with concepts or people who are positively viewed. So, let's explore the subtle dance of positive connections and see how influencers skillfully direct our perceptions and behaviors in subliminal persuasion.

4. Social Proof's Power: Have you ever noticed that we often follow the actions of others? That's social proof's magic and a major force in the realm of subtle persuasion. Let's explore this intriguing area of influence and see how the strength of data, recommendations, and testimonies can affect our choices by appealing to our innate desire to do as others do.

Imagine the following situation: you're online, deciding whether to try a new product. Then, all of a sudden, you see a label saying "Bestseller" or "Top Choice." When you realize that other people have selected these goods, it makes you feel confident. Social evidence in action! Since so many people enjoy it, you're more inclined to try it.

Another weapon in the social proof armory is testimonials. Let's say you want to find a restaurant. Reviews that highlight the food's taste and the staff's friendliness sway you because they highlight other people's positive experiences. Their recommendations constitute a type of social proof that influences your choice to try the eatery.

Celebrities who promote items make use of the social proof effect. Imagine a sports shoe being promoted by your favorite athlete. The endorsement implies that you should be able to use the shoe if it suits you. You are inclined to give a product more serious thought because you want to be affiliated with something well-liked or supported by others.

Let us now discuss the artificial consensus. Have you ever seen labels such as "Customer Favorite" or "Bestselling in the Market"? They give the impression of broad popularity even when they don't offer precise figures. Our brains interpret this as social proof, increasing our propensity to select a good or service that the majority seems to approve of.

Social proof is all about using the crowd's knowledge—it's not about mindlessly adhering to it. Investigating the mechanics of social proof is similar to taking a closer look at the minute influences on our choices. The skill of subtly persuading successfully exploits our inclination to fit in and follow the herd, influencing our decisions by demonstrating that others have already made similar decisions. So, let's explore the subtle magic of social evidence in the world of covert persuasion and break through to the magic of influencing by numbers.

5. Manipulation of emotions.

Let's now shed light on the sneaky strategies that play right to our emotions. Emotions become a playground for manipulation in the field of persuasion. We will investigate how emotions are manipulated to evoke particular feelings that result in desired effects. This isn't about playing with people's emotions; it's about learning how influencers may subtly direct people—sometimes without their knowledge—by appealing to their vulnerabilities, wants, or anxieties.

Consider a security system marketing. It might evoke feelings of uneasiness by providing a clear picture of a home that is under attack. Doing so sets off an emotional chain reaction that leads to the intended result—buying the security system for peace of mind.

Another emotional channel is desired. Think of a premium automobile marketing campaign. The story, music, and pictures could evoke prestige, success, and admiration. Influencers gently promote the notion that having a car might satisfy certain emotional demands by associating the product with these pleasurable feelings.

Vulnerability is exploited occasionally. Imagine a charity campaign highlighting the struggles endured by less fortunate people. This emotional blackmail tries to provoke compassion and a want to lend a hand. Influencers assist us in supporting their cause by appealing to our emotions.

Consider the example of a speech on politics. An effective speaker may employ emotive language to engage the listeners. They manage emotions to establish a connection and sway opinions by telling personal tales or evoking a sense of shared hardship.

It is not necessary to discount real relationships or causes to comprehend emotional manipulation. It's about realizing which instruments affect feelings to get particular results. Influencers manipulate feelings to sway decisions and perceptions, similar to how storytellers create stories to arouse emotions.

It's not about avoiding feelings as we explore the emotional terrain of covert persuasion; rather, it's about understanding how they may be shaped. It's similar to knowing the components of a recipe: influencers are the chefs creating the experience, and emotions are the tastes. Let's investigate the various levels of emotional manipulation and understand how the hidden realm of persuasion manipulates our emotions to influence our actions.

SUBLIMINAL MESSAGING

Our attention now turns to the covert practice of subliminal messaging as we continue to explore the nuances of silent dominance. This method works like a subdued lead violinist, exerting its effect just below the surface of human consciousness. In this section, we solve the enigma of subliminal messaging by removing the layers and exposing the secret techniques that subtly affect the subconscious.

Consider subliminal advertising as an expert painter delicately highlighting specific areas on a painting. It uses subtle clues and implied hints rather than big, bold strokes to paint a complex picture deep inside the mind. Without our conscious knowledge, this artwork takes shape, leaving a lasting impression on how we see and react to the world around us.

Please look at a marketing example where a company uses brief visuals or messaging in its ads. Even if these images elude conscious awareness, they are intended to be viewed by the subconscious. Exposure to these subliminal cues can shape preferences over time by subtly associating the brand with favorable feelings.

When it comes to subliminal messaging, audio components are important. Consider the subtle use of sounds that elicit particular emotions in a movie's soundtrack. Even though they are not consciously recognized, these audio cues add to the movie's overall effect and heighten the audience's emotional experience.

The field of self-improvement is another one where subliminal messaging is powerful. Imagine that you are listening to a motivational audio file that has affirmations buried deep inside the sound. The subliminal affirmations reinforce positive beliefs and attitudes subconsciously while you are consciously focusing on the primary message.

Investigating subliminal messaging is like solving a puzzle. It entails knowing the nuanced methods to smuggle recommendations past our conscious filters, including brief flashes or murmured remarks. These covert techniques, whether in self-help, entertainment, or advertising, access the subconscious mind's spoken language.

As we explore this section, awareness rather than mistrust or fear will be gained. It's like donning special glasses that make the hidden brushstrokes in the persuasive picture visible. By exposing the covert effects of subliminal messaging, we can learn more about the complex dance of silent dominance, in which invisible, delicate forces mold the subconscious. Among the several types of subliminal messaging are the following:

1. Visual Nuances: Within the field of subliminal messaging, there is a covert visual language that eludes our conscious awareness. Let's examine visual subtleties in more detail: those fleeting images, symbols, or flashes that pass too swiftly for our conscious awareness. Here, we explore influencers' strategies to deliberately place these covert images, creating traces on the subconscious that gently direct our perceptions and decisions.

Imagine that you are watching a movie, and during one scene, there is a brief glimpse of a product discreetly positioned in the backdrop. Your subconscious mind records it even if you aren't aware of it. When you're shopping, that good might strike your eye, and you might feel more tempted to consider buying it. A seed was sown in your mind by the unseen image.

To achieve visual subtlety, symbols are essential. Examine a logo design in which a tiny, discreetly inserted symbol has a deeper significance. It could convey a sense of dependability, inventiveness, or trust. When you see the sign often, even if you might not notice it immediately, it adds to your overall impression of the brand.

Another strategy is the employment of flashes. Words like "refreshing" or "quality" may appear briefly in a fast-paced advertisement; while your conscious mind may not notice them, your subconscious will. Positive words linked with that product slightly affect your perception when you think about it later.

Political campaigns also use subtle visual elements. A candidate's picture could be purposefully combined with images of a happy family or a waving flag to evoke feelings of patriotism and family values in the subconscious. These understated images have an impact on how the public perceives things.

It's not about being tricked as we navigate the world of visual subtleties but about realizing the silent power of these little details. It's similar to learning that a painting has a secret layer; even if you might not notice the intricacies, they nevertheless impact the piece as a whole. We become more conscious of how influencers intentionally employ these ephemeral images to shape our opinions and decisions without our knowledge by revealing the strategies behind visual subtlety.

2. Sound Whispers: Regarding subliminal messaging, the auditory world is filled with a silent orchestra. Now, let's explore auditory whispers, those inaudible noises, whispers, or frequencies that exist just beyond the threshold of our conscious perception. This investigation reveals how these little auditory cues—deftly concealed in background noise or music—can influence our feelings, thoughts, and actions. It's similar to unearthing a secret orchestra that composes reactions outside the realm of our conscious knowledge.

Imagine the scene from a thrilling film. Though unnoticed by you, there could be whispers or soft noises in the background that heighten the stress. These aural clues heighten your feelings during the scenario by acting on a subconscious level. The unseen impact is what gives the whole cinematic experience something more.

One effective medium for auditory subliminal messaging is music. Imagine enjoying a catchy song with affirmations gently reinforced in the lyrics. The lyrics' subliminal messages influence your subconscious and positively mold your ideas while you're actively enjoying the music.

Another aspect of auditory subtlety is frequency. Imagine a tune that promotes relaxation and contains soothing frequencies. Even though these frequencies may not be conscious, they interact with your brainwaves to induce relaxation. It is a covert invitation for your mind to relax and de-stress.

Auditory subliminal messaging in advertising can be blended with background noise or jingles. A catchy tune with a subliminal message could help consumers associate a product favorably. Your subconscious mind catches up on the message even if you aren't aware of it, gently affecting how you view the brand.

It's not about being duped as we delve into the world of aural whispers; it's about comprehending the complex ways sound shapes our perceptions. It's similar to realizing that, even though you're unaware of it, a background song influences your mood. Through deciphering auditory cues, we can reveal the silent symphony of subliminal transmission, in which sounds function as unseen puppeteers, directing our actions in ways we may not be aware of.

3. Language Embedded: Words can be more than just symbols; they can also operate as sly agents, affecting our feelings and behaviors. Let's explore embedded language, the practice of obfuscating signals in written or spoken texts. This investigation reveals the art of language subtleties, wherein hidden meanings function outside the conscious mind. It's similar to learning a secret code the subconscious interprets and uses to direct behavior without our knowledge.

Picture an audience being addressed by a motivating speaker. On the surface, such remarks encourage self-assurance and tenacity. Nevertheless, while your conscious mind is focused on the main point of your speech, these embedded phrases subtly operate on your subconscious, reinforcing positive thoughts and altering your attitude. These phrases might be subtle affirmations such as "you are capable" or "you can succeed."

Embedded language is frequently used in taglines and slogans in advertising. Look at a beauty product with a phrase like "Unleash Your Radiance." While the conscious mind recognizes the allure of radiant skin, the embedded language also gently promotes self-expression and empowerment. The product may entice you with its skincare properties and the implied promise of self-actualization.

Politicians also sway public opinion with embedded words. While intentionally focusing on their programs, candidates may frequently utilize expressions like "strong leadership" or "bright future." This helps to create good associations and enhances the public's impression of the candidate.

Embedded language can be used even in casual discussions. Say a buddy tells you to try a new restaurant, "You won't regret it; it's unforgettable." Your conscious mind processes the suggestion, but the embedded language gently shapes your expectations, building suspense for an amazing meal.

Understanding embedded language is similar to solving a puzzle's hidden message. Understanding the intricacies, tones, and subliminal clues woven throughout language is necessary. As we examine this section, the key is to recognize words' underlying power rather than doubt them. The deft application of linguistic instruments to subtly influence our behavior and thoughts, causing an effect outside our conscious awareness, is known as embedded language art.

4. Psychology of Color: Not only are colors beautiful, but they can also communicate with our minds without words. Let's explore color psychology, the subtle skill of using colors to elicit feelings, connections, and reactions. This investigation reveals the clever ways influencers manipulate color in presentations, branding, and images to evoke feelings in the subconscious. It's similar to getting a sneak peek at an influence palette, where some hues subtly direct people toward particular results.

Think about the color red. It's frequently connected to enthusiasm and vigor. Consider a fast-food restaurant incorporating red into its branding—it's not just for show. Red quietly affects your feelings, bringing in an exhilarating and urgent feeling. You may notice that you're more likely to act quickly, such as when placing an order at the counter.

Conversely, blue is associated with trust and serenity. Imagine a tech corporation with a blue logo. The color conveys a subliminal sense of stability and dependability. Your subconscious association of their items with trust may influence your decision to choose them over rivals when you see them.

Because of its brightness, yellow is frequently associated with warmth and cheerfulness. Consider a company that embodies positivity and pleasure. They employ yellow in their images for more purposes than just aesthetics. It's a calculated move to arouse emotions and establish a subliminal bond between the company and a good mindset.

Color psychology applies to designs and presentations as well. Consider a speaker discussing sustainability in a presentation that uses green. Without saying it out loud, the color reinforces the idea of being in harmony with nature and the environment. After hearing the speaker's remarks, the audience would unconsciously link her thoughts to environmental awareness.

Color psychology is the study of the common feelings that colors tend to elicit rather than the practice of concluding specific hues. It has the effect of a silent language on our emotions and choices. We have the chance to recognize the skill of influencers who, without saying a word, use color as a tool to sway our views and direct our behavior as we negotiate the nuances of color psychology.

5. Disclosed Factors in Advertising: Enter the realm of advertising, where undetectable influence is used in a game of subtle forces. This trip reveals advertisers' strategies to influence customer decisions without directly requesting consent. Advertisements carefully use subliminal cues to build subconscious associations, instilling brand loyalty and influencing our purchasing decisions. These associations may be found in anything from product packaging to pictures and slogans.

Let's dissect it. Consider yourself in a grocery shop, passing by a box of cereal. The vivid hues, well-placed symbols, and even the word arrangement on the packaging are all intended to change your opinion of the product. While you may not know every aspect, your subconscious knows these hints. It uses them to gently influence your decision to select that specific cereal over alternatives.

Consider a vehicle commercial for the moment. The advertisement's slick graphics, soothing soundtrack, and color scheme are all components of a subliminal campaign. The objective is to foster a favorable emotional connection with the brand to increase your likelihood of considering that particular car model while you're in the market.

Slogans are also effective instruments. Think about the Nike slogan "Just Do It." It conveys a message of empowerment and resolve and promotes physical exercise. This catchphrase influences your view of the company and drives your purchase decisions when you see it frequently, whether in ads or billboards.

There is more to the world of subliminal messaging in advertising than meets the eye. It's about the background noise you hear in advertisements, the subliminal affirmations a speaker uses in speaking, the hues that arouse particular feelings in people, and the invisible forces that work together to create a persuasive symphony.

As we explore the hidden aspects of advertising, it's not about being duped but appreciating the skill that goes into it. Subliminal advertising takes on the role of a silent architect, forming the context for our purchasing decisions.

CHAPTER 5
The Subconscious Mind's Power

Let's investigate The Subconscious Mind's Power in Chapter 5, which takes us into some unexplored psychological territory. Imagine an enormous pool of unrealized potential, a secret world where unseen forces shape our attitudes, convictions, and behaviors. As we explore this chapter, prepare to learn the mysteries of the subconscious, a powerful force that molds our decisions, perspectives, and sense of self. This voyage transports us to the darkest recesses of the psyche, where the subconscious plays devious tricks on the enigmatic world of human conduct with unmatched might. So, prepare for an investigation that will unveil the inner power as we solve the riddles and examine the influence of the subconscious mind on our fundamental nature.

EXPOSING THE SUBCONSCIOUS.

Our minds are made up of both conscious and unconscious activities, like complex tapestries. The subconscious mind is a strange place hidden behind this complexity. It functions covertly, outside our conscious knowledge, affecting our perception of reality, molding our actions, and ultimately defining who we are. It's similar to an undercover agent. Consider this investigation a revealing voyage, an article that lifts the veil to reveal hidden secrets within the subconscious. This huge unrealized potential pool subtly shapes every part of our lives.

Picture yourself immersed in thought while you drive a well-known road. Suddenly, you reach your goal without really recalling how to get there. That's your subconscious at work, directing your behavior with ease while letting your conscious mind stray. Think about the impact of early recollections. A certain fragrance or sound can take you back in time, which elicits feelings and actions. This subconscious is taking over and influencing your current experiences; it is not a conscious decision.

Consider your habits, such as reaching for a snack or chewing your nails under stress. The subconscious is frequently the source of these automatic reactions. Comprehending these patterns provides an insight into the subconscious's immense impact on our day-to-day existence.

Like a filter, the subconscious mind processes the vast amount of information constantly being presented to us. It chooses what commands our attention and what is ignored. Have you ever noticed how, after only learning about a word or topic, you instantly become aware of it? That's your subconscious taking it seriously at this point.

As we embark on this explanatory trip, we will see that the subconscious mind has a practical influence rather than being a supernatural entity. Uncovering its riddles leads to a deeper knowledge of the unsung hero that shapes our experiences, decisions, and understanding. Now, let's explore this further, learning about the inner workings of the subconscious mind and its diverse effects on our daily existence.

I. Abysses of the Mind: Imagine the subconscious as an iceberg, with the true action occurring beneath the surface, and what we perceive is only the tip. Join me as we explore the Depths of the Unconscious, the first layer. This is like a vast ocean that extends well beyond our conscious consciousness. Thoughts, memories, and desires reside there, silently functioning beneath the surface.

Consider a childhood incident that continues to impact your decisions to this day. It might be a persistent dread, a lesson learned, or even a reassuring memory. These events are buried deep within the unconscious, influencing your reactions without conscious awareness.

Think about your routines and habits—those you do without much thinking. Maybe the first thing you do when you wake up is reach for your phone. This conduct is rooted in the unconscious, where habits and patterns are created; it is not a conscious choice.

Now, consider your dreams. They frequently access the unconscious, bringing to light facets of our feelings and ideas that aren't usually apparent during the day. Investigating these dream environments can reveal hidden levels of the unconscious mind.

The unconscious influences our behaviors and reactions in ways we may not understand, much like a silent puppeteer. It's similar to the invisible currents that guide a ship below the water's surface in that it's where behavior roots itself. Additionally, unrealized potential and a treasure trove of experiences and ideas are waiting to be discovered within this enormous ocean of the unconscious.

The key is recognizing the invisible forces at work as we go into the unconscious. It's realizing that a complex web of memories shapes our conduct, wants, and outside forces that lie just beneath our conscious thinking. So, let us go deeper into our investigation, removing more layers to reveal the wealth of unrealized potential within the subconscious.

II. Conditioning and Programming: Now, let's explore the second layer, Conditioning and Programming. Consider the subconscious mind as rich soil in which our views and attitudes are shaped by seeds planted at a young age. This process begins with the impressions our experiences, family, and society leave behind—imprints that serve as the foundation for our deeply established behaviors.

Imagine a youngster growing up in a household that values being truthful. Truthfulness is repeatedly emphasized, which plants a seed in the subconscious's rich soil. As these youngsters get older, the importance of honesty comes naturally to them, influencing their actions without them even realizing it.

Now, consider what society expects of you. People living in a society that values perseverance and hard work greatly may find it easy to adopt these virtues. These cultural factors function as deceptive builders, helping to program and condition the subconscious.

Experiences are also very important. Consider a person who grew up with a dog and experienced happiness. Dogs may be instilled in the subconscious as sources of joy and comfort. Conversely, a bad event could trigger a conditioned reaction of avoidance or anxiety.

Consider learning a language. A youngster who grows up bilingually transitions between languages with ease. This is the outcome of the subconscious mind's conditioning and programming, which allows it to adjust to the language patterns introduced during infancy.

In this layer, the influencers—parents, teachers, peers, and societal norms—are the subtle architects. They aid in developing reflexive reactions and patterns that direct our behavior without conscious awareness. Our subconscious brains are like a fertile ground where influences have left their mark, shaping our behaviors like an invisible set of rules.

It is important to comprehend how these early impacts turn into the unseen builders of our behaviors when we examine programming and conditioning. It acknowledges that our subconscious guides us in ways we may not be aware of on a conscious level. Now, let's continue our trip, dissecting the layers to uncover the complex training and programming that creates the template for our automatic reactions.

III. Dream Language in Symbols: Let's investigate the symbolic language of dreams, the third layer. As the stories, your subconscious mind tells you while you sleep, imagine dreams. These nighttime experiences reveal insights into your inner workings through symbolic communication. Your subconscious creates stories as you sleep, expressing feelings, wants, and unresolved problems through symbols and metaphors.

Think about a dream in which you are falling. This popular sign could stand for a dread of failing or a feeling of losing control. The act of falling is your subconscious's way of expressing a feeling or experience that you're having trouble with in the here and now.

Envision having a dream in which you fly. This could represent a wish to be free or avoid restrictions. Even while you might not soar above the skies while awake, the symbolic language of your dreams expresses your desire for freedom.

Imagine now that you are being hunted in a dream. This may suggest that you are under pressure or feeling pursued in your waking life. Dream symbolic language reflects feelings you may need to be more aware of during the day.

Dream analysis takes on the structure of deciphering a hidden message. Every person has a distinct symbolic language, and deciphering the symbols might reveal more about the inner workings of your mind. Your subconscious guides you, encouraging you to discover facets of yourself that the everyday grind may have obscured.

Think about dreams that keep coming back. A worry of not being adequate or a circumstance in which you feel unprepared in real life may be indicated if you frequently dream about being unprepared for an exam. Your subconscious is alerting you to particular features of your inner world through the symbolic language of these recurrent dreams.

It's not about being a dream expert as we explore the Symbolic Language of Dreams, but rather realizing that your dreams have deep significance. Gaining a grasp of the symbolic language allows you to understand yourself better, and it's similar to having a private conversation with your subconscious. Let's now move to explore, dissecting the layers to understand the fascinating stories your subconscious mind creates while you dream.

IV. The Power of Habits to Influence: Let's investigate the symbolic language of dreams, the third layer. As the stories, your subconscious mind tells you while you sleep, imagine dreams. These nighttime experiences reveal insights into your inner workings through symbolic communication. Your subconscious creates stories as you sleep, expressing feelings, wants, and unresolved problems through symbols and metaphors.

Think about a dream in which you are falling. This popular sign could stand for a dread of failing or a feeling of losing control. The act of falling is your subconscious's way of expressing a feeling or experience that you're having trouble with in the here and now.

Envision having a dream in which you fly. This could represent a wish to be free or avoid restrictions. Even while you might not soar above the skies while awake, the symbolic language of your dreams expresses your desire for freedom.

Imagine now that you are being hunted in a dream. This may suggest that you are under pressure or feeling pursued in your waking life. Dream symbolic language reflects feelings you may need to be more aware of during the day.

Dream analysis takes on the structure of deciphering a hidden message. Every person has a distinct symbolic language, and deciphering the symbols might reveal more about the inner workings of your mind. Your subconscious guides you, encouraging you to discover facets of yourself that the everyday grind may have obscured.

Think about dreams that keep coming back. A worry of not being adequate or a circumstance in which you feel unprepared in real life may be indicated if you frequently dream about being unprepared for an exam. Your subconscious is alerting you to particular features of your inner world through the symbolic language of these recurrent dreams.

It's not about being a dream expert as we explore the Symbolic Language of Dreams, but rather realizing that your dreams have deep significance. Gaining a grasp of the symbolic language allows you to understand yourself better, and it's similar to having a private conversation with your subconscious. Let's now move to explore, dissecting the layers to understand the fascinating stories your subconscious mind creates while you dream.

V. Emotional Stockpile: Now, let's explore the Emotional Reservoir, the sixth layer. A basic aspect of human nature, emotions are stored in the subconscious as an emotional vault. See it as a reservoir where repressed feelings, desires, and fears smolder beneath the surface, subtly affecting our responses and molding our experiences as aware beings.

Consider a time when you were quite upset about something that didn't seem like much. The emotional reservoir may be the source of this strong emotional reaction. It can be a long-suppressed emotion that comes to the surface and influences your current behaviors without realizing it.

Think about an illogical fear. Maybe you fear heights; the idea of being atop a big building makes you shudder. This fear could have been discreetly held in the emotional bank due to a past event or a recollection of your early years, affecting your reactions.

Now, picture the happiness you get from returning to a treasured memory. The emotional reservoir also produces that cozy, nostalgic sense. This is also where happy feelings are kept, waiting to improve your life and boost your general well-being.

Investigating the subconscious's emotional terrain is akin to plunging into a large ocean of emotions. It offers perceptions of the subtleties that support your mental health. It's admitting that a reservoir of emotions influences your life's story just below the surface of your conscious consciousness.

To sum up, your subconscious mind actively participates in your everyday events rather than merely a passive observer. The subconscious mind is a living region just waiting to be explored, containing the depths of the unconscious, the programming and conditioning that molds your beliefs, the symbolic language of dreams, the influencing power of habits, and the emotional reservoir within. By revealing the hidden forces that shape the emotional story of your life's journey, unraveling its secrets helps you better understand who you are. Let's now carry on with our investigation, removing the layers to reveal the complex emotional dance that takes place inside the deep domain of the subconscious mind.

THE SUBCONSCIOUS MIND'S INFLUENCE ON DECISION-MAKING.

A significant finding as we further study the subconscious mind is its potent influence on judgment. The intricate webs woven across the subconscious are crucial, profoundly influencing our decisions in ways that may not always be obvious at first glance.

Let's dissect the subtle influence of the subconscious on judgment and examine its practical workings.

Consider a situation when you had to make a choice, such as selecting between employment offers or determining what to have for supper. While your conscious mind weighs advantages and disadvantages, your subconscious is also at work, using emotions, patterns learned from the past, and experiences.

Think about a job interview. Your subconscious may impact your confidence by drawing on prior achievements or failures, while your conscious mind concentrates on answering inquiries and showcasing your abilities. Without your conscious knowledge, the subliminal undercurrents of your subconscious influence the impression you convey.

Consider choosing a holiday destination. Your subconscious may push you toward a place that brings back pleasant memories or feelings, even if you're unaware of it. Your conscious mind considers things like preferences and budget.

The subconscious influences decision-making like a knowledgeable guide subtly offering advice in your ear. It helps you make decisions by utilizing a large library of stored data, including emotional reactions, cultural influences, and prior experiences.

Think about your tendencies when making decisions. Subconscious patterns developed from previous encounters with social influence and teamwork may have shaped your tendency to consult others before making decisions.

Rather than voicing its ideas overtly, the subconscious mind quietly infiltrates decision-making processes. Gaining insight into this dynamic allows us to see why we make our own decisions. Recognizing the quiet orchestrations operating beneath the surface is as important as considering the obvious variables.

This invites us to acknowledge the collaboration between our conscious and subconscious thoughts as we examine how the subconscious influences decision-making. It's admitting that your decisions are influenced by a complicated interaction between your subconscious guide's whispers and cognitive analysis. Peeling back the layers, let's continue our exploration to learn more about this complex dance in decision-making.

1. Gut instincts and intuition: Your subconscious can especially communicate with you when making decisions—through gut instinct and intuition. Consider it a mild prod, utilizing all of the wisdom and insights you have amassed over the years. These imperceptible cues are vital in directing your decisions. Trusting these intuitive cues can help you make judgments that align with deeper ideas stored in your subconscious, even though they might not always come with a clear explanation.

Imagine attending a job interview and knowing that the organization might not be a good fit, even though you meet all the requirements. While your conscious mind can examine the job description and benefits, your subconscious may subtly communicate with you based on unconscious preferences or past experiences.

Consider selecting a residence. After visiting a few possibilities, one may seem to fit all the rational requirements, while another seems appropriate. That sensation, sometimes referred to as a "gut instinct," is your subconscious influencing your choice by considering elements that are not immediately apparent.

Imagine that you are meeting someone for the first time, and either you click with them right away or you sense something is wrong. Your intuition is a subconscious tool that processes nonverbal cues, memories of past interactions, and emotions to form an initial impression.

It's like drawing from a hidden wellspring of knowledge when you follow your gut. Acknowledging that your intuition might provide insightful information rather than discounting reasoned analysis is important. They are the outcome of your subconscious making sense of a tonne of data and offering a "shortcut" to making decisions.

Paying attention to your intuition can make a huge difference in everyday situations, such as selecting between two job offers or determining whether to attend a specific event. It directs you toward decisions that align with your deeper understanding, like an internal compass.

Thus, as we examine the function of gut instinct and intuition in decision-making, we must accept these imperceptible cues as important partners. It's an admission that your subconscious is an ally in helping you make decisions consistent with who you are, thanks to its abundance of gathered knowledge.

2. Emotional Factors: Let's now investigate the second factor, emotional influences. Deeply ingrained in your subconscious, emotions significantly influence how you make decisions. Emotions subtly influence your choices, whether the thrill of a fresh start, the dread of failing, or the security of comfort. Making decisions with greater balance and reason is possible when you know these underlying emotional currents.

Consider starting a new career. Even if a new opportunity offers growth and fulfillment, your decision may be influenced by your fear of leaving a stable employment. Recognizing this anxiety enables you to assess the choice with greater objectivity.

Think about purchasing a home. Practical considerations sometimes take a backseat to the joy of discovering a location that seems like home. By recognizing the emotional pull, you may compare the emotional connection to other considerations, such as location and pricing.

Now consider how comfortable routine is. When making a decision that requires you to move away from well-known routines, your subconscious feelings may oppose the change. Understanding this emotional impact allows you to determine whether following the routine is helpful or only a reaction to familiarity and comfort.

Emotional factors are similar to silent allies when it comes to making decisions. They influence your perception of possibilities and can impair your judgment. But by recognizing these feelings, you may make decisions with a greater sense of clarity about what your actual priorities and objectives are.

Consider choosing a professional route. Being conscious of these sensations enables you to make decisions that are in line with your long-term objectives rather than impulsive impulses, such as when you're feeling excited about a new task or afraid of not living up to expectations.

Emotions come into play in daily decisions, from choosing what to have for dinner to making important life decisions. Acknowledging their impact is like possessing a compass directing you across the emotional terrain, guaranteeing your choices align with your current emotions and overall goals.

Therefore, we must recognize these guiding principles when we learn more about the emotional factors that drive decision-making. It's realizing that feelings, although necessary, might occasionally take you down routes that might not align with your goals. Gaining this understanding will enable you to make choices that are in line with your short- and long-term goals. Let's investigate further, removing more layers to see how emotions maneuver through the complex domain of the subconscious.

3. Identification of Patterns: Let's now discuss the third factor, Pattern Recognition. Like a pattern investigator, your mind is skilled at identifying well-traveled routes based on prior encounters. It functions like a mental file system, allowing you to make decisions based on past experiences. Although this natural ability might make decisions easier, it's important to be conscious of potential biases and make sure that decisions take into account the particular circumstances of each case.

Think of an instance where you've interacted well with someone from a similar background. Your subconscious may help you connect with others who naturally fit that pattern by recognizing patterns in their behavior. It's important to realize, though, that this realization may inadvertently cause one to miss out on important opportunities to form relationships with others from diverse backgrounds.

Consider having to make decisions concerning your financial investments. Your subconscious may gravitate towards comparable choices if you have favorable encounters with a specific investment approach. To make sure your choice isn't based only on historical trends, it's important to strike a balance between this and a mindful awareness of the potential hazards and the state of the market now.

Consider selecting a restaurant at this point. If you've enjoyed eating at a particular restaurant, your subconscious may steer you in that direction. On the other hand, keeping an open mind about new experiences guarantees that you will take advantage of unique dining opportunities and undiscovered treasures.

Identifying patterns is like having a trustworthy helper swiftly filtering through prior encounters to provide well-traveled routes. It simplifies decision-making by referencing prior successes. However, it's critical to combine this automatic ability with deliberate thought, particularly when specific circumstances diverge from well-known patterns.

Finding patterns in daily choices, such as choosing projects or employing staff, can save time. However, being aware of such biases guarantees that choices are well-rounded and consider the particular subtleties of each circumstance. Hence, when we explore the function of pattern recognition, we must respect this innate ability and exercise caution to make judgments that are as context- and nuance-aware as feasible. Let's investigate further, removing more layers to comprehend the complex dance of decision-making in the subconscious.

4. Biases in cognition: Let's examine cognitive biases, the fourth layer, next. These operate similarly to subconsciously ingrained mental shortcuts that may inadvertently affect how you make decisions. These biases, which include availability heuristic, anchoring, and confirmation bias, affect how you process information and make decisions. It is imperative to become aware of these biases to reduce their possible impact and make more objective decisions.

Think about confirmation bias, which is the tendency for your subconscious to favor information that validates your preexisting ideas. When choosing between two possibilities, you may unconsciously ignore data that contradicts your preference and place greater weight on information that supports the option you are leaning toward.

Consider anchoring, a bias in which the first piece of information you are given unintentionally shapes your decisions. Consider negotiating a pay where the initial offer acts as an anchor that impacts your idea of a reasonable or acceptable wage range.

Now consider the availability heuristic, in which your subconscious makes decisions based on information that is easily accessible to it, frequently gleaned from recent experiences. Even if there are other good options, you could be more likely to choose a specific brand again if you've had a nice experience.

These biases are similar to unseen forces influencing how you make decisions. Being conscious of them is essential to ensuring your selections are as unbiased and well-informed as possible, even if they're natural and frequently act as effective mental shortcuts.

Consider the addition of a new member to the team. You may ignore important traits or abilities if you're unintentionally swayed by a single piece of information or the first impression. Being conscious of anchoring bias allows you to step back and think about the bigger picture.

Cognitive biases are present in everyday activities, from financial decisions to groceries. Gaining awareness is similar to donning glasses to improve your vision when making judgments. This enables you to avoid potential biases and make decisions that align with your preferences.

Thus, when we explore the topic of cognitive biases, it is important to recognize these imperceptible factors that affect your decision-making process. It's admitting that even while your subconscious is quite effective, it can occasionally mislead you. Your instrument for making decisions that are more objective and consistent with your true preferences is awareness. Let's continue our investigation to learn more about how the subconscious mind handles decision-making complexities.

5. Unconscious Pursuit of Goals: Let's investigate Unconscious Goal Pursuit, the sixth layer. Like a covert mission operative, your subconscious frequently pursues objectives without your conscious knowledge. This hidden work of striving subtly directs decision-making toward results consistent with underlying goals. Understanding these implicit objectives can help us better understand the motivations behind our decisions.

Consider your professional or academic decisions. Your subconscious may subtly direct you toward a particular career path due to underlying objectives like financial security or personal fulfillment. You can better match your choices with your inner ambitions by recognizing these subtle cues.

Think about your relationships. Unstated objectives in your mind could have to do with trust, friendship, or common ideals. These objectives gently direct your decisions, influencing choices that result in deep connections that satisfy your emotional requirements.

Now, consider your personal growth. Your subconscious may encourage you to develop particular traits, learn new things, or develop new abilities. Recognizing these unspoken objectives allows you to make choices that advance your ongoing development and satisfaction.

Pursuing unconscious goals is similar to having a compass pointing toward your dreams, even if you aren't aware of them. Consider deciding to pick up a new skill or pastime. Your subconscious objectives may be guiding you toward pursuits that satisfy your need for enjoyment and self-actualization.

In day-to-day living, subconscious goals influence decisions on leisure activities and habits to develop. Deciphering the hidden code that directs your decisions and identifying these goals will help you make decisions that align with your inner wants.

As we explore the idea of unconscious goal pursuit, it becomes clear that the key is recognizing your subconscious's silent architect. It's realizing that, even when conscious awareness isn't there, your mind actively pursues objectives that enhance your fulfillment and meaning in life. Increasing your understanding of this will enable you to make decisions consistent with the underlying goals that form the story of your life. Let us extend our exploration by removing further layers to comprehend the complex dance of goal pursuit in the deep domain of the subconscious.

6. Triggers for Memories: Subconscious memories can influence decisions by acting as triggers. Unconsciously, decisions might be influenced by positive or negative associations that are connected to prior experiences. Analyzing these memory triggers makes it possible to assess results and implications with greater knowledge.

Realistically speaking, it's critical to recognize how the subconscious influences judgment. Knowing these nuanced dynamics—caused by memory triggers, emotional effects, cognitive biases, pattern identification, intuition, or unconscious goal pursuit—improves one's capacity to make thoughtful judgments in various life contexts.

As we end our investigation into how the subconscious influences our ability to make decisions, we are left to navigate the unseen currents that influence our choices. The subconscious, a storehouse of feelings, desires, biases, patterns, intuition, and memories, subtly yet profoundly affects how our decisions turn out.

Recognizing the subconscious's influence on decision-making becomes useful for navigating the invisible forces at work. We reveal the complex threads that impact our decisions, from trusting our gut feelings to identifying emotional influences, being aware of cognitive biases, comprehending unconscious goal pursuit, and investigating memory triggers.

Let us leave this chapter with a heightened awareness and understanding that our subconscious plays a role in our judgments and that they are not only the result of reasoned deliberation. This insight allows us to navigate the mental undercurrents with fresh clarity and make more deliberate, thoughtful, and conscious decisions.

We carry on this self-discovery journey with every choice we make, revealing the factors that mold our course by removing the layers of the subconscious. Anticipate more insights into the subtle arrangements within the maze of the human mind in the upcoming chapter. May the knowledge acquired here clear the path and enable us to make choices with discernment, awareness, and a stronger sense of the subtle currents inside.

CHAPTER 6
Exploitation And Cognitive Bias

This chapter explores the murky areas of the complex field of human psychology where cognitive biases and manipulation collide. Imagine a place where people quietly exploit people's weaknesses and employ psychological tricks to their advantage. Prepare yourself for the manipulation that results from the intricate interplay of cognitive biases as we delve into the less well-known realm of quiet influence in this chapter. As we negotiate the complex terrain of human behavior, it becomes increasingly important to comprehend how these biases might be exploited.

EXPLOITATION AND COGNITIVE BIASES.

An important first step in understanding exploitation and cognitive biases is identifying the common biases that influence our actions and perceptions without being obvious. These prejudices, which frequently function subconsciously, are used as manipulative instruments by individuals aware of their influence. Let's explore the terrain of common biases and reveal the deceptive agents that thread the veins of human consciousness.

1. Confirmation Prejudice:

Confirmation bias, among the most widespread biases, influences our propensity to look for, analyze, and retain information that supports our preconceived notions. Understanding this bias entails being aware of our tendency to favor data that supports our beliefs and actively searching out opposing viewpoints to balance this innate tendency.

2. Bias in Anchoring: When we base our decisions unduly on the first piece of information we come across, or the "anchor," we are sinning anchoring bias. It is necessary to critically examine the first information offered and deliberately reevaluate its impact on later decisions to identify this bias. Understanding anchoring enables us to make more unbiased and knowledgeable decisions.

3. Heuristic for Availability: We overvalue information that is easily accessible to us due to the availability heuristic. Acknowledging this bias entails recognizing our propensity to base decisions on current or readily available information. Seeking out additional information proactively aids in overcoming the constraints imposed by the availability heuristic.

4. Overconfidence Prejudice: Overconfidence bias takes hold when people overestimate their skills or the integrity of their opinions. Self-awareness and being willing to reevaluate our confidence levels are necessary to acknowledge this bias. Getting input from others and considering different perspectives helps lessen the influence of overconfidence bias while making decisions.

5. Retrospective Bias: The "I-knew-it-all-along" phenomenon, also known as hindsight bias, is the tendency to believe that events are predictable after they have happened. Acknowledging this bias is being aware of how foresight differs from retrospect and using caution when extrapolating judgments about the past. An effective way to combat hindsight bias is to reflect on the uncertainty in forecasts actively.

6. The Framing Effect: The framing effect illustrates how information presentation can affect how decisions are made. Awareness of how information is presented and realizing that even small alterations in language or context can influence opinions is necessary to identify this bias—examining how information is framed closely aids in developing more impartial judgments.

To successfully navigate the world of exploitation and cognitive manipulation, it is imperative to comprehend and recognize these common biases. We give ourselves the ability to make decisions that are less prone to manipulation and more resistant to minor effects by becoming aware of our cognitive vulnerabilities. Exploiting these biases and defense mechanisms against their deceptive manipulations will be discussed in more detail in the next sections.

TAKING ADVANTAGE OF COGNITIVE BIASES.

Within the shadowy field of dark psychology, knowing how manipulators make money by taking advantage of cognitive biases reveals the complex tactics used for one's benefit. The unseen masterminds behind these tricks take advantage of the weaknesses in human thought processes. Let's examine the ways that dark psychology uses cognitive biases to its advantage to create a subtle yet powerful web of influence.

1. Creating Conceptions: Confirmation bias is a clever tool used by dark psychology to skew perceptions. Manipulators build a skewed reality that supports their story by providing people with information that confirms their preconceived notions. They can control the narrative and shape people's impressions without the people they are influencing recognizing that they are being deliberately manipulated.

2. Affecting the Making of Decisions: Anchoring bias turns into a weapon used by dark psychologists to sway judgment. They can influence opinions and direct people toward decisions that support the manipulator's goals by deftly introducing an opening fact (the anchor). They can sway decisions in their favor because of their control over the process.

3. Manipulating Emotions: The availability heuristic is exploited by dark psychology to control people emotionally. Manipulators produce long-lasting impressions that impact behavior in the future by setting up circumstances that elicit powerful emotions and ensuring these emotional experiences are easily retrieved from memory. Dark psychologists find that manipulating emotions can be a powerful tool in their toolbox.

4. Taking Advantage of Overconfidence: Dark psychologists create a false sense of assurance to take advantage of people's overconfidence bias. Persuasive communication is frequently used, giving the impression of competence or inspiring unjustified confidence in their story. Manipulators use the overconfidence bias as a technique to gain the trust and control of their targets.

5. Changing Storylines: It takes talent to exploit hindsight bias to influence narratives. Dark psychologists exploit people's propensity to see things as predictable after they happen. Manipulators can rewrite history by creating stories that support their bias, affecting how people view their intentions and actions.

6. Establishing Mental Frameworks: Dark psychologists possess a potent tool in the framing effect. They mold people's cognitive frames of perception through deliberate framing of material to evoke particular emotional responses or biases. They can manipulate ideas, change attitudes, and control the narrative through this clever framing.

Dark psychology is a complex dance of exploitation and cognitive biases that depends on its capacity to take advantage of the subtle weaknesses in the human psyche. People can avoid becoming victims of these covert strategies by being aware of how manipulators shape perceptions, affect decision-making, emotionally manipulate, take advantage of overconfidence, manipulate narratives, and construct psychological frames. The following section will cover how to protect yourself against these manipulations and keep a watchful attitude when dealing with negative psychological influences.

We stand at the nexus of awareness and resilience as we wrap up this chapter on cognitive biases and exploitation. The exploitation of cognitive weaknesses is a fertile ground for dark psychology, which skillfully manipulates perceptions, decisions, and emotions without requiring our conscious consent.

By identifying how manipulators use our cognitive biases, we enable ourselves to traverse the shadows carefully. This knowledge is a barrier against the covert plots of people trying to exploit the weak currents in our thoughts.

Let us take the understanding that awareness is the antidote to manipulation with us as we proceed. We strengthen our mental defenses by being aware of how perceptions are shaped, how they affect decision-making, how emotions are manipulated, how overconfidence is exploited, how narratives are manipulated, and how psychological frames are created.

The path through the darkness requires resiliency and ongoing learning. We shall examine defense mechanisms against the deceptive tactics of dark psychology in the upcoming chapter. Equipped with consciousness and an alert mentality, we begin out on a course that enables us to successfully negotiate the complex dance between the good and the bad in human conduct.

CHAPTER 7
Strategies For Manipulating Relationships

The chapter delves into the art of manipulating relationships. Even while relationships are generally good, let's talk about the negative aspects, namely, how they can be manipulated. We'll concentrate on useful strategies applied in social situations when trust, feelings, and vulnerabilities are turned into control instruments.

Consider this chapter an exploration of the workings of Relationship Manipulating Techniques. Good relationships depend on trust, which can be manipulated to the manipulator's advantage. Our shared emotions, or emotions, can be skillfully manipulated to steer relationships in a specific direction. Every relationship has vulnerabilities, which are used for power.

This investigation is not about poetic concepts but rather a realistic look at how people employ certain strategies to manipulate relationships' dynamics quietly. We'll explore particular techniques illuminating how manipulators employ these instruments to mold and manage the dynamics within the intricate web of connections. Get ready for a thorough investigation designed to assist you in recognizing and fending off the deceptive pull of manipulation on the relationships that shape our existence.

MANAGING EMOTIONS IN PARTNERSHIPS: HANDLING THE TRICKERY LANDSCAPE.

To manage the direction of a relationship, people who practice emotional control purposefully manipulate the emotions of others. This technique, which manipulators frequently employ, tries to accomplish particular goals or preserve a power dynamic in the relationship.

Fundamentally, emotional control is about influencing the emotional terrain to obtain the upper hand. Manipulators may purposefully fabricate situations or use strategies to arouse their victims' particular feelings. Depending on the manipulator's goals, these feelings might contain anything from happiness and affection to fear, rage, or melancholy.

Positive reinforcement techniques like affection, praise, or awards might be applied to encourage loyalty and obedience. On the other hand, strategies that arouse guilt, fear, or play on vulnerabilities help seize control and increase the other person's vulnerability to the manipulator's influence.

Maintaining successful relationships requires an understanding of emotional regulation. It necessitates paying more attention to emotional changes that seem contrived or out of proportion to the circumstances. Real emotional experiences and mutual understanding are the foundation of healthy relationships; emotional control brings manipulation and undermines authenticity and trust.

Emotional intelligence development is essential to empowering oneself against emotional domination. Protecting mental health entails being aware of one's feelings, seeing deceptive behavior, and setting clear boundaries. By developing self-awareness and resilience, people can successfully negotiate the challenging terrain of emotional regulation in relationships, resulting in connections based on mutual understanding, authenticity, and trust.

POWER RELATIONS IN INTERPERSONAL RELATIONSHIPS.

Analyzing power dynamics in interpersonal relationships provides insight into how influence is distributed and manipulated in these relationships. Power dynamics largely determine a partnership's distribution of authority, decision-making, and control.

Power dynamics frequently become a technique manipulators use to establish their authority. They recognize how influence is used to obtain the upper hand, whether explicitly or covertly, which is essential to understanding these dynamics. To gain or hold onto power, manipulators may employ various strategies, including agenda-setting, information control, and vulnerability-exploiting.

Withholding information, for instance, can be used as a tool in a power struggle where one person manipulates the knowledge of the other to affect their opinions and choices. Establishing the agenda entails guiding the discussions or actions to support the manipulator's goals. One way to exploit vulnerabilities is to target emotional flaws or insecurities to keep control.

Managing power dynamics calls for a sophisticated comprehension of the forces at work. It entails spotting warning indications of imbalance, probing the reasons behind particular actions, and setting sound limits to prevent manipulation. Mutual respect, honest communication, and shared decision-making are the foundations of healthy partnerships; therefore, it's critical to identify and correct any imbalanced power dynamics. The objective as we examine this facet is to provide people with the knowledge and skills necessary to manage power dynamics in a way that promotes real, harmonious relationships.

As this chapter which explores the nuances of Relationship Manipulating Techniques, ends, the trip through the complexities of human connections reveals both potential for progress and problems.

The ability to identify emotional control, comprehend power dynamics, and maneuver around deceptive tactics are all essential for maintaining positive relationships. The way forward is to use this knowledge to foster relationships based on mutual understanding, authenticity, and trust.

Let these insights be your compass as we move into the next chapter, assisting you in navigating the delicate dance of relationships with resilience, awareness, and the discernment to separate the real from the fake in the relationships that impact our lives.

CHAPTER 8
Techniques For Behavioral Conditioning: Dissecting Our Influences

Greetings, and welcome to Chapter 8, where we explore Behavioral Conditioning Techniques. To put it plainly, we are investigating how our behavior can be molded and impacted. Consider it as knowing the strategies and instruments that, frequently unseen, direct human behavior.

Similar to puppeteers manipulating strings, specific methods can gently direct our actions. This chapter examines these tactics in more detail and reveals how external factors shape our decisions, behaviors, and responses. So grab a seat and explore how our behavior is subtly conditioned and how awareness can guide us.

CONDITIONING TO SHAPE BEHAVIOR.

Let's dissect how our conduct is shaped clearly and concisely. It functions similarly to training, just for routine activities that we are unaware of.

1. Constructive Encouragement: Consider the concept of positive reinforcement, such as receiving points for excellent deeds. For instance, your teacher may give you a gold star or commend you for finishing your homework. Your positive emotions motivate you to continue completing your assignments.

2. Rewarding Neglect: Negative reinforcement now refers to actions taken to prevent unpleasant experiences. To get rid of your mom's bothersome reminders, picture yourself cleaning your room. You're more likely to clean up again once you've cleared the area and avoided the pestering.

3. Penalties: Punishment might take the shape of a consequence that indicates, "Hey, that wasn't okay." For example, you might lose screen time or other privileges if you neglect your tasks. It teaches you what's appropriate.

4. extinction: When a habit reaches extinction, it's because it's losing its appeal. Suppose in the past, you used to yell to attract your mother's attention. You may decide to cease creating it if she begins to ignore the noise because it is no longer effective.

Knowing these techniques enables us to recognize how we are guided without realizing it. As we explore these subtle forces impacting our behavior throughout this chapter, let's find out how they function in our daily lives.

PAVLOVIAN EFFECTS:

Now, let's talk about something called "Pavlovian Influences." This term may sound sophisticated, but it simply refers to how certain cues or signals can subconsciously influence our habits.

Consider a scientist who researched dogs by the name of Pavlov. He rang a bell each time he fed them. The dogs eventually began to identify the bell with food, so even in the absence of food, they would salivate at the sound of it.

It occurs in our lives as well. A signal is when your phone buzzes to tell you you have a message. You've eventually realized that buzzing indicates you've received a message. Therefore, the buzz may prompt you to check your phone immediately, even while you're occupied.

Recognizing these Pavlovian effects enables us to understand better how unconsciously formed habits might be by specific triggers. So, be mindful of those small bells in your life, and let's learn more about how they subtly affect our daily behaviors.

We establish analogous associations in our habits, just as the dogs trained by Pavlov did when they heard the bell. For example, if you consistently eat during the show, your brain associates snacking with TV time. Therefore, even if you're not hungry, your brain may signal to crave a snack when you settle down to watch a show.

Knowing these factors is like having superpowers when forming our habits. We can alter the cues connected to a habit to break it. On the other hand, we can establish unambiguous cues to aid in forming new habits.

Consider your daily schedule in the morning. You could start your day with coffee every time. The aroma of coffee turns into a wake-up signal. The aroma of coffee can serve as a cue to stretch in the morning, which will help the new habit stick if you decide to incorporate it into your routine and do it immediately after drinking your cup of joe.

Not only are Pavlovian influences present in our everyday lives but they are also utilized in advertising. Have you ever noticed how some logos or jingles instantly conjure up images of a particular brand? That is the outcome of cues being deftly used to establish associations and shape our decisions.

CHAPTER 9
The Dark Sides Of Communication

Now, let's shed some light on "The Dark Side of Communication," which, despite its enigmatic title, is about realizing the negative effects concealed in our communication. It consists of the following items:

1. Deceptive Words and Expressions: People can use words to influence others rather than to express themselves. It's similar to employing deceptive language to influence someone's thoughts or emotions. For example, imagine a commercial saying, "Limited time offer – act now!" The words are chosen to create a sense of urgency, encouraging you to make a quick decision.

2. Subtle persuasion: Have you ever noticed how certain advertisements make you want something you didn't even consider before? That's subtle persuasion at play. It's about using images, colors, or sounds to create a desire for a product or idea. Like a movie scene making you crave popcorn – it's not a coincidence; it's intentional.

3. Emotional appeals: The dark side also involves tugging at your emotions to get a response. Advertisements, speeches, or even social media posts might use sad stories or happy moments to make you feel a certain way. Once you feel connected emotionally, you might be more likely to agree with what's being said or buy into an idea.

Understanding these dark communication tactics is like putting on a pair of glasses that reveals hidden influences. As we explore the dark side, watch for these communication tricks and see how they quietly affect our thoughts and choices in everyday situations.

VERBAL MANIPULATION:

Now, let's dive into "Verbal Manipulation." It might sound like a big term, but it's all about understanding how words can shape our thoughts, sometimes in ways we might not even notice. They include the following:

1. Loaded Language: Loaded language is like using words that carry extra weight or emotion. It's not just about expressing a thought; it's about making you feel a certain way. For instance, instead of saying someone "disagrees," you might hear they "strongly oppose." The words chosen add intensity and emotion to the message.

2. Euphemisms: Have you ever heard someone say something that sounds nice but means something that could be better? That's a euphemism. It's using pleasant words to soften a harsh reality. For example, instead of saying "fired," someone might use a euphemism like "let go" to make it sound less negative.

3. Double-Speak: Double-speak is like saying something to confuse or mislead deliberately. It's using words that sound good but might mean little. Politicians sometimes use double-speak to make things sound positive even when they might not be—for instance, calling a policy "revenue enhancement" instead of a tax increase.

Recognizing verbal manipulation helps us see through the words meant to guide our thoughts. So, as we explore this topic, pay attention to the language used around you and uncover how it can quietly influence how you perceive things.

NON-VERBAL DECEPTION.

Now, let's uncover the world of "Non-verbal Deception." It sounds mysterious, but it's all about understanding how people communicate without saying a word, and sometimes, it involves tricking or misleading others.

1. Body Language: Body language speaks volumes without using words. For example, if someone avoids eye contact, they might hide something or feel uneasy. On the other hand, open and relaxed body language can signal honesty and comfort.

2. Facial Expressions: Faces can reveal a lot about what someone is thinking or feeling. A smile might indicate happiness, but a forced smile might hide discomfort. Observing subtle shifts in facial expressions can aid in discerning the genuine emotions underlying the spoken words.

3. Microexpressions: Have you ever seen a quick facial expression that seemed out of place? Those are microexpressions. Tiny, involuntary movements that reveal genuine emotions. Detecting these fleeting signals can uncover hidden feelings.

4. Gestures and Posture: Gestures, like waving or pointing, and posture, how someone holds themselves, convey a lot. Leaning in might show interest while crossing arms can signal defensiveness. Paying attention to these silent movements helps you read between the lines.

5. Tone of Voice: Even when words aren't misleading, the way they're said can be. The tone of voice, including pitch and speed, can convey emotions or intentions. For instance, a sarcastic tone might say one thing, but the words mean another.

6. Proxemics: This is about personal space and how close people stand or sit. Invading personal space might make someone uncomfortable while standing too far away can signal aloofness. Understanding these invisible boundaries adds another layer to non-verbal communication.

7. Eye Movements: Where someone looks can reveal hidden thoughts. Avoiding eye contact might indicate discomfort or dishonesty, while direct contact often signals confidence or sincerity. Understanding these subtle eye movements adds another layer to non-verbal communication.

8. Touch and Haptics: Touch is a powerful non-verbal signal. A pat on the back can convey support, while a firm handshake might signal confidence. However, touch can also be deceptive – a seemingly friendly touch might hide underlying motives.

9. Clothing and Appearance: How someone dresses and presents themselves can also convey messages. A sudden change in appearance or dressing in a certain way might be an attempt to project a specific image or hide something.

10. Microgestures: In the world of non-verbal communication, micro gestures are like hidden whispers. These tiny movements, like a slight nod or a quick eyebrow raise, can convey subtle meanings that might escape verbal expression. They're the secret codes that add depth to our understanding.

11. Paralinguistics: Beyond words, paralinguistics covers aspects like pitch, intonation, and rhythm in spoken language. A change in pitch can signify excitement or nervousness, while alterations in rhythm might indicate emphasis or urgency. Unraveling these vocal nuances provides insights into the emotional undercurrents.

12. Silence and Pauses: Sometimes, what isn't said speaks volumes. Deliberate silences or well-placed pauses can be strategic, creating emphasis, signaling discomfort, or even serving as a deceptive tactic. Understanding the art of silence adds another layer to decoding non-verbal communication.

As we delve deeper into the intricate world of non-verbal communication, keep an attentive gaze on these subtle cues. They form an unspoken language that shapes our understanding and sometimes conceals intentions beneath the surface. Let's continue this journey to uncover the intricacies of human interaction.

Exploring non-verbal communication is like navigating a silent language. Keep a keen eye on these nuanced signals in your interactions, and let's uncover more about how non-verbal communication shapes the way we understand and sometimes deceive each other.

HOW NON-VERBAL COMMUNICATION SHAPES OUR UNDERSTANDING AND DECEPTION

Now, let's break down how non-verbal communication impacts how we get to know each other and sometimes play tricks.

1. Reading Emotions: Think of non-verbal signals as a secret code for feelings. Someone's face, gestures, or tone can tell you a lot about what's going on inside their head. It's like understanding the hidden language of emotions without needing words.

2. Creating Impressions: Imagine you're meeting someone for the first time. Their posture, how they dress, and even their handshake send signals. It's like they're painting an impression without saying a word. But here's the trick – sometimes, people deliberately craft these signals to create a specific image.

3. Deceptive Signals: Now, here's where it gets interesting. Non-verbal cues can also be used to deceive. Someone might smile, but their eyes tell a different story. Paying attention to these mixed signals helps you see beyond what's shown on the surface.

4. Building Trust: Non-verbal cues, like maintaining eye contact and open body language, play a crucial role in building trust. When someone appears sincere and consistent in their non-verbal signals, it contributes to the establishment of trust in relationships.

5. Cultural Nuances: Different cultures have unique non-verbal communication norms. What a friendly gesture in one culture could be misunderstood in another. Navigating these cultural nuances adds complexity to how we interpret non-verbal signals.

6. Power Dynamics: Non-verbal communication often reflects power dynamics in a conversation. Posture, gestures, and even personal space can signify who holds authority. Recognizing these cues helps decipher the subtle power play in various interactions.

7. Mirroring and Synchrony: In positive interactions, people tend to mirror each other's non-verbal cues. This synchrony creates a sense of connection and understanding. However, in deceptive situations, individuals might intentionally mimic gestures to create a false sense of rapport.

So, as we explore the topic more, remember that it's not just about understanding; it's also about decoding the subtle ways people can trick or mislead using gestures, expressions, and tones. Stay tuned to unravel more about the fascinating dynamics of human interaction.

EMOTIONAL EXPLOITATION THROUGH LANGUAGE.

Emotional exploitation through language is like a subtle dance where words become the puppeteer, manipulating emotions and perceptions. It's a phenomenon deeply woven into human interaction, often harnessed for various purposes – be it in personal relationships, marketing strategies, or even political discourse.

1. The Art of Persuasion: At its core, emotional exploitation through language is an art of persuasion. Words are carefully chosen to evoke particular emotions, connecting the speaker or writer with the audience. Think about advertisements that use heartwarming stories to sell a product. The goal is to make you feel certain, influencing your decision-making process. Consider political speeches; leaders use emotionally charged language to rally support or gain empathy. The choice of words can evoke a sense of unity, fear, or hope, strategically shaping public opinion. It's a language dance aimed to sway emotions and, in turn, affect conduct.

2. Creating Empathy and Connection: Emotional exploitation through language is partly about building empathy and connection. When someone shares a personal tale or utilizes familiar language, it forges a link with the audience. This relationship is potent, especially in storytelling or persuasive communication. Think of how impactful it is when a speaker says, "Imagine if you were in this situation." By evoking empathy, language becomes a potent instrument for persuasion.

In personal relationships, emotional exploitation through words can take a worse turn. Manipulative individuals may use emotionally charged phrases to influence or gaslight others. By exploiting vulnerabilities or phobias, they obtain an upper hand in interpersonal dynamics.

3. The Dark Side: Gaslighting and Manipulation:

Gaslighting is emotional manipulation that involves influencing someone into questioning their sanity or views. This is performed by sophisticated language strategies, such as denial, deception, or twisting facts. The purpose is to create uncertainty and confusion, making the victim more open to manipulation.

Manipulative language can also be evident in toxic relationships where one person utilizes guilt-tripping, humiliating, or emotional blackmail to manipulate the other. Phrases like "If you loved me, you would..." or "You always make everything about you" can be instruments of emotional exploitation, creating a power dynamic that erodes the victim's self-esteem.

4. The Role of Marketing and Media: In marketing and advertising, emotional exploitation through language is a well-honed craft. Advertisements draw emotions to sell things, making customers link a certain brand with positive sentiments. Consider how a simple slogan like "Because you're worth it" can establish a sense of self-esteem and drive customer choices.

News providers also employ emotional language to gain attention and shape impressions. Headlines that elicit fear or fury grab more viewers, illustrating how language can be powerful in shaping public opinion.

5. Navigating the Nuances: Understanding emotional exploitation through language is vital for individuals to manage the intricacies of communication. It requires being aware of the emotional triggers buried in words, identifying manipulative strategies, and developing resilience against emotional manipulation.

In conclusion, emotional exploitation through language is a diverse component of human communication. While it may be a force for positive connection and persuasion, it also harbors a darker side of manipulation and control. Navigating this language terrain requires awareness, critical thinking, and a grasp of how words may impact emotions and behaviors.

CHAPTER 10
Unseen Behavioral Control

Get ready to explore "Unseen Behavioral Control" as we unearth the unseen threads that impact our behavior without noticing. Imagine being in a puppet show, but the strings are invisible. In this chapter, we'll go deeply into the unseen factors that subtly influence our behavior, thought processes, and decision-making. It's similar to learning about the master puppeteers of our conduct behind the scenes. Let's get started and reveal the unseen forces that direct our behavior.

SUBTLE INFLUENCES IN SOCIAL ENVIRONMENTS.

As we progress through "Unseen Behavioral Control," we reveal the strings that subtly direct us. We went from comparing it to being in a puppet show with invisible strings in the introduction to social circumstances when these invisible influences influence our behavior without our knowledge.

1. Normative Social Power: Recall the rules we discussed earlier, the invisible ones. Social standards operate similarly to the behavior of backstage directors. They serve as the unwritten rules instructing us on appropriate behavior in various settings, such as libraries and sports arenas. These standards subtly shape our behavior without anyone clarifying our expectations.

2. Group Behavior: Group dynamics exert a strong pull on us as we navigate social environments. Imagine it as a magnetic force in which all acts affect each other. The group's energy influences us more than we know, whether applauding at a concert or keeping silent at a conference.

3. Social Proof in Practice: Adding to this is the concept of social evidence, which holds that we should base our decisions on what other people are doing. This is the crowd's unseen effect. We are inclined to join in when everyone appears to be enjoying it. That new restaurant with the enormous lineups outside? In action, it's social evidence.

4. Simulating Action: Have you ever noticed that you were unconsciously mimicking someone else's behavior? That's imitating, which happens frequently in social situations. We synchronize our behavior with those around us by unintentionally imitating those we like or admire.

5. The Power of Authority: As we proceed, we see the impact of authority in social contexts. Some people are more powerful than others, and we follow their example. Our brains are programmed to pay attention to people who appear to have authority, so it may be a teacher, a supervisor, or just someone who exudes positivity.

6. Unspoken correspondence: If you go further, you'll find the realm of unspoken communication. Not just words spoken in social situations. Body language, tones, and facial expressions can communicate ideas without words. Our concealed language shapes our reactions.

7. The Art of Subtle Persuasion: Persuasion is subtle and works in the background, influencing us subtly. For example, advertisers manipulate our emotions using colors, music, and images; we don't even realize this is happening. Persuasion is in action, subtly urging us in one way or another.

8. The Impact of Cultural Background: Referring back to our opening, several cultures have their subtle influences. BehaviorCultural standards shape behavior; hence, what is deemed courteous in one society may not be in another. Comprehending these factors enables us to move through social situations with awareness and respect.

9. Peer Influence and Its Results: As we continue to investigate, peer pressure appears as an unseen force in social settings. Our decisions are subtly influenced by the opinions of our peers, which occasionally cause us to make decisions we otherwise would not have made. Knowing how peer pressure affects us allows us to make decisions consistent with our ideals.

In the large-scale work "Unseen Behavioral Control," social environments are the canvas on which these imperceptible currents weave our behavior. These unseen factors, which include authoritative figures, social standards, and the deft art of persuasion, greatly impact human behavior without our conscious knowledge. Understanding these subtleties helps us navigate social situations more effectively because we can perceive the hidden forces at work.

PSYCHOLOGICAL WARFARE TACTICS.

Deeper into the maze of "Unseen Behavioral Control," our investigation skillfully transitions from the murky world of psychological warfare strategies to the delicate influences in social contexts. Just as we've seen the unseen forces at work or in our relationships, knowing psychological warfare strategies reveals a more purposeful and frequently hidden aspect of power.

1. Social Environments: Looking back over our journey thus far, we understand that social environments are not just places where subtle influences occur but also act as a breeding ground for more deliberate psychological strategies. The social dynamics, group dynamics, and unspoken communication that we have studied serve as the stage upon which tactics are implemented.

2. Knowing How to Use Psychological Warfare: It's important to clarify what we mean by psychological warfare before getting into techniques. This is not a phrase from the battlefield but refers to the strategic application of psychological tricks to control or sway people or organizations. It's the skill of taking advantage of weaknesses, causing misunderstandings, and influencing opinions to accomplish particular goals.

3. As a Psychological Technique, Gaslighting: Building on the prior discussion of gaslighting, let's examine it as a psychological ploy. Gaslighting is gently leading someone to doubt their truth or sanity. This strategy aims to induce skepticism, uncertainty, and reliance on the manipulator. An essential first step in reducing the effect of gaslighting is recognizing it.

4. Emotional Mismanagement and Abuse: Psychological warfare goes beyond emotional manipulation to include the strategic use of emotions. Emotions become manipulation tools, whether used to provoke fear, rage, or sympathy. Emotional manipulation is a method that politicians, advertisers, and even people can employ to further their objectives.

5. Control and Isolation: Isolation is another psychological warfare method. Manipulators increase their power by cutting people off from their networks of support. This can be accomplished more obviously by severing social ties or more covertly restricting access to information. Isolation becomes a potent weapon to increase a person's susceptibility to influence.

6. Warfare using Propaganda and Information: As we enter the information sphere, propaganda becomes apparent as a psychological warfare strategy. Propaganda, whether distributed via social media or traditional media, seeks to sway public opinion by presenting incomplete or false information. Navigating the contemporary information landscape requires an understanding of the workings of propaganda.

7. How to Cause Cognitive Dissonance: Psychological warfare frequently takes advantage of cognitive dissonance or the unease from contradictory thoughts. Manipulators cause discomfort to force people to reconcile the disparity in a way that advances their goals. This strategy makes use of people's innate need to find internal consistency.

8. Subliminal Communications: Regarding our talk about subtle persuasion, psychological warfare employs subliminal messaging more strategically. Subtle communications that fall below the conscious awareness threshold can affect behavior without the subject's knowledge in various contexts, including politics, advertising, and interpersonal manipulation.

9. Making Use of Individual Variations: Psychological warfare techniques frequently take advantage of the individual disparities in the psychological basis that we have examined. Manipulators use individual personality features, vulnerabilities, or past experiences to customize their approaches and increase their effectiveness.

10. Defying Psychological Assault: Comprehending psychological warfare methods is critical, but it's just as necessary to investigate counterstrategies. Developing strong social ties, media literacy, and critical thinking abilities are effective barriers against psychological manipulation.

Acknowledging these strategies enables people to fight back and safeguard their mental health.

In conclusion, the intricacy of covert behavioral control becomes increasingly evident as we move from the subtle effects in social contexts to the purposeful strategies of psychological warfare. Recognizing these strategies is the first step to navigating the shadows of influence, which include emotional manipulation, gaslighting, isolation, propaganda, and more. The path continues as we arm ourselves with the knowledge to fend off deception and protect our mental liberty.

CHAPTER 11
Ethical Considerations

Welcome to Chapter Eleven, where we delve into "Ethical Considerations," a vital component of our journey. Think of influence as a potent instrument, similar to a compass that directs decisions. Let's now discuss how to use this tool sensibly and act morally.

1. The Greatest Duty of Persuasion: It feels like a big duty when we have an impact on other people. Imagine being able to influence people's thoughts and actions. It sounds strong. The catch is that we must exercise caution when using this ability. Ethics can assist us in making these decisions by guiding us toward what is just and moral.

2. The Boundary between Persuasion and Trickery: Ethics enables us to distinguish between deceiving someone and convincing them. When we are convinced, we act as amiable advisors, imparting knowledge and assisting others in making decisions. However, when we deceive, it's like guiding someone along an unclear route. Understanding this distinction and ensuring that we remain on the correct side are the main topics of this chapter.

3. Informing Others of the Situation: Consider ethics as being truthful and transparent in our actions. This is known as informed consent in the influence community. It entails ensuring that individuals are aware of the influences on them. Transparency makes things better for everyone in politics, advertising, or even casual conversations with friends.

4. Honoring Individual Freedom of Choice: Ethical influence is comparable to honoring an individual's right to free will. It's saying, "You get to decide." Picture yourself in charge of your choices, free from undue pressure from others. Letting people make their own decisions free from pressure is the goal.

5. Avoiding Causing Damage to Others: One crucial ethical guideline is never to injure another person. Being an ethical influencer means not harming people or exploiting their shortcomings. Ensuring that no one is harmed in the process is the goal of all endeavors, whether sales, group leadership, or simple friendliness.

6. Juggling Everyone and Me: Everyone is considered by ethical influence, not just myself. It's similar to striking a balance between my interests and everyone else's. Our goal when exerting influence is for everyone to win and come out ahead. It's the moral thing to do.

7. Being Truthful and Transparent: Being truthful and forthright is a powerful tool in the field of ethics. When exerting influence over someone else, we ought to be transparent about our goals and methods. In this approach, trust can develop, and everyone knows what is happening.

8. Ethics Changes With Us: We are reminded in this chapter that ethics are subject to change. It evolves together with our surroundings. The ethical influence changes in response to new technology, diverse cultures, and shifting views. This ensures that we act morally in the world we live in.

Still in Chapter eleven, let's discuss using influence wisely. It's about treating a buddy with kindness and fairness when leading them through a difficult route. As we venture into the ethical aspects of our path, let us always remember that making the right decision significantly impacts our influence and the environment we live in. As we explore invisible behavioral control, let's explore the wonders of ethical considerations.

THE MORAL DILEMMA OF DARK PSYCHOLOGY.

As we enter the core of our investigation into "Ethical Considerations," the road becomes clear and presents a big obstacle: the moral problem of dark psychology. It's similar to coming to a fork in the road where our decisions significantly impact our moral compass. As we delve deeper into the intricacies of Dark Psychology and the ethical choices that lie ahead, let's continue our investigation.

1. The Complex Dance of Negative Psychology: As we have already discussed, Dark Psychology is the enigmatic aspect of influence. Here, the dance gets complicated because the attraction of invisible control is irresistible. We consider decisions that could put us on a path where good and wrong are hazy while standing on the precipice of an ethical tightrope.

2. The Secret Allures: In the field of Dark Psychology, the need for control is frequently concealed. It begs the fundamental question: Is it morally permissible to exercise influence covertly without drawing attention to oneself? The attraction of covert power emerges as a major motif, luring us to investigate the influence's shadows.

3. Manipulation and Respect in Balance: We must contend with the conflict between manipulation and respect as we work through this moral quandary. There is a propensity to manipulate others to further one's interests. On the other hand, the ethical basis of respect gives people the freedom to make their own decisions. Finding equilibrium in this delicate equilibrium is the difficult part.

4. Moral Thoughts on the Effect: Think about how our decisions affect other people in the context of Dark Psychology. The greater the harm that manipulation could inflict, the more difficult the moral quandary becomes. It carefully analyzes whether pursuing control is worthwhile given the possible drawbacks for individuals impacted.

5. The Boundary of Ethics Between Coercion and Persuasion: The distinction between force and persuasion is more obvious in the shadows. Determining whether our influence softly persuades or veers into coercion is the crux of the moral quandary. It carefully analyzes the strategies used and how they affect ethics.

6. Entices and Unethical Manoeuvres: Dark Psychology exposes the propensity to use cunning strategies like deceit, manipulation, and terror. The moral problem emerges when we consider the propriety of employing such tactics, considering that Playing with emotions and well-being has ethical ramifications.

7. The Ethical Conflict Between Fair Play and Self-Interest: Imagine for a moment a game where we must choose between fair play and self-interest. Dark psychology frequently emphasizes self-interest, which intensifies the conflict between ethics. The crux of the conflict is whether succeeding at the expense of others is consistent with a vision of justice and integrity.

8. Vision into Long-Term Repercussions: We look into the future while our trip takes shape. Beyond our decisions now, the moral problem forces us to consider the long-term effects of adopting Dark Psychology. It's a reflection on whether our choices create a society where justice and trust survive or if they pave the way for a less favorable future.

Here we are, navigating Dark Psychology's moral terrain. Our decisions in this problem determine our course and add to the moral fabric of the world we create. Let knowledge, empathy, and a dedication to moral leadership guide us over this difficult terrain as we explore the hidden domains of behavioral control.

RESPONSIBLE USE OF PSYCHOLOGICAL KNOWLEDGE.

Our journey toward comprehending the appropriate application of psychological knowledge shifts as we navigate the complex terrain of Dark Psychology. Finding an ethical decision-maker in the sphere of influence is akin to finding a lantern in the dark. Together, let's explore this area and find a way to apply psychological findings responsibly and thoughtfully.

1. **Understanding as a Two-Sided Sword**: Consider psychological knowledge as an effective and adaptable instrument. In the field of Dark Psychology, having this knowledge can have unintended consequences. It gives us the ability to comprehend human behavior on the one hand, but it also creates the temptation to abuse that understanding for one's benefit. Here's where accountability comes into play.

2. **Increasing Awareness to Empower Others:** Being aware is the first step toward responsibility. The ethical use of psychological knowledge is dedicated to enlightening and empowering others. It lets people see and comprehend the forces

influencing their ideas and behaviors, like turning on the lights in a dark room. When knowledge is disseminated ethically, it can lead to enlightenment.

3. Education's and transparency's roles: Think of transparency and education as the cornerstones of responsible use. Here, the focus is openly exchanging psychological knowledge without ulterior motives. Transparency is a barrier against the improper application of psychological insights by teaching people about the concepts of influence and the techniques used.

4. Developing Critical Thought: Fostering critical thinking is part of being responsible. It's similar to providing eyewear for everyone to see past possible manipulations. Promoting critical thinking, analysis, and assessment of information makes people more adept at navigating the influence terrain. Psychological understanding thus turns into an instrument of empowerment rather than control.

5. Practical Boundaries of Ethics: Ethical boundaries act as checkpoints in the correct application of psychological knowledge. It has to do with appreciating individual autonomy and limits. Violating moral standards by infringing on privacy or using dishonest tactics is considered a violation of accountability. This lays the foundation for applying psychological discoveries conscientiously and ethically.

6. Juggling Persuasion with Deference: Respect and persuasion are like delicate balances. When used responsibly, persuasion seeks to educate, direct, and motivate decisions that align with people's welfare. It respects the freedom of decision and stays away from manipulation. This equilibrium guarantees the ethical application of psychological knowledge, creating an atmosphere where influence is a constructive force.

7. Moral Guidance and Persuasion: Leadership is not exempt from responsibility. Within Dark Psychology, moral leaders know how their actions affect others. They set an exemplary example by responsibly using psychological knowledge. As a beacon, ethical leadership enables people to use their understanding of human behavior for beneficial and productive endeavors.

8. Impact and Legacy Over Time: The long-term effects are taken into account while using psychological knowledge responsibly. It's about creating an ethical influence legacy that will endure for generations. Ethical psychologists recognize that their decisions now influence how people interact with one another and the larger story of social well-being.

Let's think of psychological knowledge as a compass that guides us away from the traps of Dark Psychology. Taking responsibility for our actions makes sense and guarantees that the knowledge we acquire is applied thoughtfully and carefully. Let accountability be the soundtrack to the complex dance between influence and expertise, guiding our movements and establishing a morally sound voyage through the hidden domains of behavioral control.

We are on the verge of an ethical horizon as we wrap up our investigation into the moral problem of dark psychology and the appropriate use of psychological knowledge. This chapter has been a voyage through lights and shadows, negotiating the nuances of influence and the decisions that mold our relationships.

During our investigation, we faced the attraction of covert control and the moral tightrope between manipulation and deference. We discussed the effect on other people and the fine line that separates persuasion from compulsion. The temptations of unethical behavior influenced our reflections, the conflict between self-interest and fair play, and the thought of long-term effects. As we approach the end of this chapter, let's condense our knowledge into a meaningful statement in the following points:

1. Duty as the guiding principle: The idea of responsibility is central to our investigation. It appears as the lighthouse beaming moral decisions across the complex dance of Dark Psychology. Taking responsibility for psychological knowledge and realizing its ability to influence thoughts and actions compels us to use it carefully.

2. The Transparency and Education Light: Education and transparency prove to be strong allies in our ethical journey. Their light dispels the shadows of deception and creates an atmosphere of empowerment and knowledge for everyone. By openly exchanging psychological expertise and educating others, we help create an environment where awareness is a barrier against unwarranted influence.

3. How to Convince While Maintaining Respect: The fine balance between respect and persuasion is evidence of ethical influence. A responsible application of psychological knowledge aims to strike a balance between a strong regard for personal autonomy and the ability to persuade. Influence becomes a constructive factor in this equilibrium, directing decisions without crossing the line into manipulation.

4. Leading in the Ethical Environment: We also talked about the importance of moral leadership in our investigation.

Setting moral guidelines is the duty of leaders, both in the public and private domains. They become lights that point others toward moral behavior in positions of influence by setting an example of responsible psychological knowledge usage and leading with integrity.

5. Legacy and Extended Effects: Let's think about our legacy as we come to an end. Ethical professionals recognize that decisions made now have an impact on the future. Leaving a legacy of moral influence is pledging to make a constructive impact on people's lives as well as the welfare of society.

To sum up, this chapter has provided insights into the ethical application of psychological knowledge while navigating dark psychology's moral minefield. Let the ethical horizon direct our decisions as we go into the upcoming chapters of our investigation. This will guarantee that our power is not merely a dance of shadows but a melodic harmony that promotes a society of dignity, self-determination, and moral decision-making. Brace up as we journey into the next chapter, where we will learn to strengthen our minds against the wrong use of dark psychology.

CHAPTER 12
Building Up Mental Sturdiness

Our journey now shifts from the moral complexity of Dark Psychology to the liberating realm of mental toughness. It's like coming out of the shadows into the light when vulnerability gives way to resilience. Building mental toughness is the cornerstone for negotiating the hidden domains of behavioral control, just as the responsible application of psychological knowledge forms the ethical foundation.

1. Accepting Resilience Following Ethical Analysis: We've gone on a sophisticated investigation of the concepts of influence, ethics, and accountability. Now, picture mental toughness as the protector that materializes during a brief period of ethical contemplation. The mental fortification equips us to bravely and resolutely confront the complex dance of influence.

2. From Perception to Self-Empowerment: After delving into the ethical implications, it makes sense to move on to developing mental resilience. Empowerment begins with the awareness that arises from the responsible application of psychological knowledge. It involves using information to strengthen the mind's internal fortitude and act as a barrier against manipulating forces.

3. Boosting the Armor of Psychology: Think of mental toughness as the psychological defense we put in place to protect ourselves from outside influences. This armor takes on new meaning in the ethical world, representing grit, resiliency, and an uncompromising dedication to one's well-being. Instead of isolating ourselves, we should arm ourselves with the tools necessary to negotiate the influence environment confidently.

4. Adaptability in the Face of Manipulation: After ethical issues are taken into account, resilience shows itself as a potent defense against possible manipulation. It's like resisting the flow of influence with confidence because one's moral decisions have given one a strong base. Vulnerability is balanced with resilience, which turns setbacks into learning experiences.

5. Adversity's Mental Gymnastics: Participating in the mental acrobatics of adversity is essential to developing mental resilience. It's taking on obstacles head-on, being flexible, and developing an outlook that makes the most of bad circumstances. People with this resilience can deal with life's ups and downs without resisting outside pressure.

6. The Lessons of Ethical Leadership: Think of the knowledge gained from moral leadership as the foundation for mental toughness. Ethical leaders exemplify resilience in the face of moral quandaries. They inspire others who want to strengthen their mental landscapes because of their capacity to overcome obstacles while adhering to moral values.

7. Being Mindful as a Strengthening Foundation: When building mental resilience, mindfulness stands out as a key component. It involves paying attention to our surroundings, being self-aware, and being in the moment. People who practice mindfulness can better understand moral subtleties and make decisions that support their mental health and moral principles.

8. Individual Development Within Ethical Frameworks: Developing mental resilience is linked to personal development. The ethical groundwork established in earlier chapters serves as a rich environment in which resilience might grow. It involves more than just enduring adversity; it also entails leveraging obstacles to spur growth and better comprehend oneself.

In this chapter, we explored a fortification expedition, strengthening our mental fortitude in response to the ethical issues previously discussed. Let mental resilience be the compass that leads us through the complexities of influence as we proceed, cultivating a mindset that not only endures outside demands but also flourishes in the pursuit of moral and empowered living.

IDENTIFYING AND DEFENDING AGAINST MANIPULATION.

As we continue exploring mental robustness domains, we address the crucial ability to recognize and counteract manipulation. See this as hardening our psychological fortress walls, arming ourselves to recognize tiny cues, and bolstering our resistance to unwelcome influence.

1. The Alert Sentry: The first step in creating mental resilience is awareness, like having a watchful guard at the entrance to our minds. Recognizing the tiny signs and the whispers of influence that try to get through are the first steps towards identifying manipulation. Being aware serves as our first line of defense, enabling us to recognize when outside influences are trying to influence our decisions and behaviors.

2. Exposing Declusive Strategies: Think of mental toughness as the tool that pulls back the curtain on manipulation's deceitful strategies. It entails being aware of the many tactics, such as guilt trips and emotional appeals. Equipped with insights gleaned from moral introspection, people can expose these strategies, diminishing their ability to shape conduct.

3. Using Your Intuition as a Guide: Intuition becomes a guiding principle in the process of building mental resilience. It's that intuitive sense, the inner compass alerting us when something isn't morally right. When one believes in one's intuition, it becomes a strong defense mechanism that helps one navigate the influence environment with increased discernment.

4. Delineating Limits as a Defense tactic: Imagine defining boundaries as building sturdy walls around our mental stronghold. It entails setting boundaries, identifying when influence crosses an uneasy zone, and adamantly claiming independence. By creating a boundary that is difficult for manipulative forces to penetrate, setting boundaries turns into a proactive defensive tactic.

5. Examining Intentions and Motives: Gaining mental resilience necessitates having an acute sense of goals and motivations. It's the capacity to determine whether outside factors support one's well-being or whether there's a hidden agenda. People can guard against deception and make wise decisions by critically analyzing the intentions underlying persuasive efforts.

6. Looking for Different Viewpoints: Consider mental toughness as a tower offering a broad perspective as it climbs above the terrain. Seeking out different viewpoints turns into a way to protect yourself from exploitation. People's comprehension expands as they examine different views, making it harder for manipulators to take advantage of limited opinions.

7. Building Emotional Hardiness: The armor that protects against deceptive strategies that target emotions is emotional resilience. It entails building a solid emotional foundation, awareness of one's emotional triggers, and creating coping skills. People with emotional resilience can resist being manipulated emotionally and react steadily and composedly.

8. Using Ethical Guidelines as Protective Barriers: As a result of being developed in the furnace of appropriate psychological knowledge application, ethical norms serve as barriers against manipulation. People can use these values as a reference point when faced with moral problems, strengthening their resistance to deceitful influences. When persuasive attempts are made, ethical grounding serves as a strong defense.

As one seeks to recognize and protect against manipulation, mental toughness becomes a powerful barrier. The borders of autonomy create an effective defense system, the walls of awareness, and the sentries of intuition. Let mental toughness be our ally as we traverse the influence landscape; it will protect our thoughts from deception and enable us to make decisions that align with our well-being and core beliefs.

BOOSTING PSYCHOLOGICAL BARRIERS

As we proceed toward mental robustness, the emphasis now switches to enhancing psychological barriers or fortifying the mental walls that protect our thoughts from outside stimuli. See these obstacles as strong gates that are difficult to breach, protecting us against evil influences and bolstering our dedication to moral decision-making.

1. Building Critical Thinking Capabilities: Developing critical thinking abilities is the first step toward overcoming psychological obstacles. It's similar to honing your analytical, questioning, and information-scraping skills. Being able to recognize the logical consistency of persuasive attempts and make well-informed decisions is made possible by critical thinking, which serves as a defense against manipulative strategies.

2. Improving Knowledge of Media: Media literacy has become a valuable tool in strengthening psychological barriers in the digital age. It entails identifying prejudice, comprehending the subtleties of information distribution, and figuring out the deceptive strategies used in various media. Improved media literacy enables people to make informed decisions while navigating the information world.

3. Increasing Confidence in Oneself: Imagine self-assurance as a wall that is reinforced inside the mental castle. Increasing self-assurance serves as a defense against deceptive efforts to make one doubt one's abilities. A strong sense of self protects the person from strategies to cause self-doubt or exploit vulnerabilities.

4. Defying Social Pressure: One way to strengthen psychological barriers is to withstand social pressure. It's similar to erecting a wall to block the impact of the masses. Even in the face of cultural expectations, people with high psychological barriers can remain autonomous and make decisions based on their principles rather than giving in to peer pressure.

5. Accepting Intelligent Emotions: Psychological barriers are guarded by emotional intelligence. It's the capacity to comprehend, control, and feel other people's emotions. People who embrace emotional intelligence can respond to emotional manipulation with composure and thoughtfulness, identifying when emotions are being manipulated and navigating it with perseverance.

6. Cultivating Presence and Mindfulness: Visualize the psychological castle surrounded by a moat of attentiveness. Being attentive means paying attention to thoughts and feelings without allowing them to influence you readily. Being mindful helps one to resist making snap decisions and reacting erratically to manipulative forces.

7. Building a Network of Support: Building a network of ethically aligned persons who support one another is essential to boosting psychological barriers. This network is a source of strength and confirmation when faced with manipulative forces. When people are supported, they act as a collective barrier against outside forces trying to pull them from their moral core.

8. Taking Advice from Previous Experiences: Resilience in psychological obstacles is built using lessons from the past. It's the capacity to learn from past experiences with manipulation, spot trends, and modify defenses as necessary. People who grow from their mistakes become skilled at seeing and thwarting deceitful approaches.

9. Determining Your Objectives: Establishing specific goals for oneself serves as a guide inside the mental fortress. When someone has clear objectives, they have a path, which makes it difficult for manipulators to take them off course. When personal goals are clear, psychological barriers are strengthened, and decisions are made with long-term aims rather than letting short-term factors sway them.

Let every facet of our psychological defenses strengthen our mental castle as we bolster it. A strong defense against manipulation can be formed by building self-confidence, improving media literacy, cultivating critical thinking abilities, and engaging in mindfulness practices. May our psychological barriers act as defenders in the complex dance of influence, keeping our decisions firmly grounded in moral values and individual welfare.

Let us conclude this chapter with a call to action: let's actively participate in strengthening our thoughts. May the citadel of mental sturdiness be our shelter and compass as we proceed through the complex world of Dark Psychology. Let our determination to erect strong psychological barriers prove our commitment to moral decisions and living a life consistent with our core beliefs.

CONCLUSION

We have ventured into the depths of the human psyche on our trip through the complexities of Dark Psychology. As we draw this investigation close, let's discuss several important concepts that have influenced how we perceive unconscious behavioral control, subconscious influence, and silent dominance.

1. The Awareness's Power: The concept of consciousness lies at the heart of our investigation. The cornerstone for traversing the shadows of Dark Psychology is comprehending the manipulative techniques, being aware of the subtle signs, and being alert to unseen forces.

2. The Compass of Ethical Considerations: A compass that guides the complex dance of influence is the ethical concern. Utilizing psychological knowledge responsibly emphasizes the value of integrity in the exercise of influence and becomes both a moral requirement and a defense against the dangers of manipulation.

3. Developing Mental Robustness: Building mental toughness is an effective approach to address the issues raised by Dark Psychology. Fortifying the mind against manipulative forces requires resilience, strengthening psychological barriers, and cultivating critical thinking.

4. Knowledge-Based Empowerment: Our path has shown us that empowerment comes from knowledge. Gaining insight into the psychological workings, the historical foundations of manipulation, and the complexities of human behavior enable people to move discernibly through the shadows.

5. Using Mindfulness in Making Decisions: The ability to be mindful becomes a valuable tool while making decisions. A barrier against rash decisions is created by being mindful, in the moment, and sensitive to one's feelings. This encourages making morally sound decisions in the face of conflicting influences.

6. The Relationship Between Ethics and Influence: The intricate relationship between ethics and influence highlights the complexity of dark psychology. Navigating the shadows requires striking a balance between persuasive strategies and moral standards, highlighting the significance of moral leadership and responsible decision-making.

7. Constant Development and Adjustment: The path through Dark Psychology is characterized by constant growth and adaptability rather than stagnation. Lifelong pursuits requiring constant dedication and introspection include strengthening psychological barriers, embracing ethical principles, and developing mental toughness.

8. The Citadel of the Resilient Mind: Finally, picture the mind as a strong fortress. Enabled by information, reinforced by moral values, and strengthened by consciousness, this fortress protects against hidden behavioral control. Let your dedication to making moral decisions serve as the foundation for a life that aligns with your ideals.

May the knowledge acquired serve as a beacon of light in the shadowy world of Dark Psychology, where subliminal influence dances its complicated dance and silent dominance looms. Let the lessons we've learned serve as tools for resilience, empowerment, and moral living when we emerge from these shadows into a world where invisible forces of influence always try to sway our actions.

PROMOTING ETHICAL BEHAVIORS IN PSYCHOLOGISTS.

It is critical to stress and encourage ethical behavior in studying Dark Psychology, particularly psychology. Let us illuminate the significance of ethical behavior for psychologists as we make our way through the shadows and reveal the mysteries.

1. The Psychologist's Ethical Compass: The most important thing is to make ethics the psychologist's compass. The foundation of responsible psychology work is ethical behavior. Psychologists have a moral code that puts the rights, dignity, and well-being of the people they work with first.

2. Educated Consent as the Basis: Getting informed consent becomes essential to encouraging moral behavior. Psychologists have a responsibility to respect people's autonomy and their right to make educated decisions about their treatment by providing them with comprehensive information on the nature, goals, and possible hazards of psychological therapies.

3. Keeping Secrets as a Sacred Trust: A fundamental trust in the psychotherapist-client connection is confidentiality. Maintaining client anonymity is essential to establishing trust and creating a space where people feel comfortable discussing their concerns. Psychologists need to take extra precautions to protect their clients' privacy.

4. Openness in Research Procedures: For psychologists who conduct research, openness is essential. Open and honest communication about research methodology, biases, and conclusions ensures the integrity of the scientific process. It takes transparency in research methods to advance knowledge morally.

5. Utilizing Influence Responsibly: With the material covered in Dark Psychology, psychologists must use their power cautiously. It is crucial to avoid manipulative strategies and ensure that whatever impact they have is in line with moral standards. Psychologists need to be aware of the possible effects that their words and deeds may have on other people's well-being.

6. A Lifelong Devotion to Advancement in the Profession: Encouraging moral conduct necessitates a lifetime dedication to career advancement. Psychologists facing difficult ethical decisions should seek supervision or counsel, participate in ongoing learning, and stay current on changing ethical standards. Psychologists can move through the shadows with skill and moral discernment if dedicated to continuing their professional development.

7. Diversity and Cultural Competence: For psychologists, acknowledging and honoring cultural diversity is fundamental to moral conduct. Understanding and appreciating each client's experiences, viewpoints, and backgrounds is essential to culturally competent treatment. Psychologists must practice inclusive and culturally aware therapy.

8. Promoting Ethical Standards: Psychologists must promote and preserve moral principles in the larger psychology community. This entails actively engaging in conversations regarding moral principles, contributing to the creation of moral regulations, and cultivating a work environment that places a premium on moral behavior.

9. Recognition of Power Dynamics: Psychologists need to understand the power dynamics in their interactions with clients. Important ethical considerations include:

- Avoiding exploitation.
- Attempting to maintain a balance of power.
- Ensuring clients feel empowered throughout their therapeutic journey.

In summary, encouraging ethical behavior in psychologists involves more than just following rules; it also entails a dedication to the welfare of the people they assist. Let ethical behavior serve as the cornerstone as we uncover the mysteries of dark psychology, guiding psychologists into the shadows with honesty, empathy, and a profound regard for the moral precepts that underpin their field.

How great this journey has been. It's great to know you stayed till this point. I'm certain that with the knowledge explored so far, we can now better use the knowledge of Dark Psychology for our own good.

THE SUBCONSCIOUS MIND'S INFLUENCE ON DECISION-MAKING.

A significant finding as we further study the subconscious mind is its potent influence on judgment. The intricate webs woven across the subconscious are crucial, profoundly influencing our decisions in ways that may not always be obvious at first glance. Let's dissect the subtle influence of the subconscious on judgment and examine its practical workings.

Consider a situation when you had to make a choice, such as selecting between employment offers or determining what to have for supper. While your conscious mind weighs advantages and disadvantages, your subconscious is also at work, using emotions, patterns learned from the past, and experiences.

Think about a job interview. Your subconscious may impact your confidence by drawing on prior achievements or failures, while your conscious mind concentrates on answering inquiries and showcasing your abilities. Without your conscious knowledge, the subliminal undercurrents of your subconscious influence the impression you convey.

Consider choosing a holiday destination. Your subconscious may push you toward a place that brings back pleasant memories or feelings, even if you're unaware of it. Your conscious mind considers things like preferences and budget.

The subconscious influences decision-making like a knowledgeable guide subtly offering advice in your ear. It helps you make decisions by utilizing a large library of stored data, including emotional reactions, cultural influences, and prior experiences.

Think about your tendencies when making decisions. Subconscious patterns developed from previous encounters with social influence and teamwork may have shaped your tendency to consult others before making decisions.

Rather than voicing its ideas overtly, the subconscious mind quietly infiltrates decision-making processes. Gaining insight into this dynamic allows us to see why we make our own decisions. Recognizing the quiet orchestrations operating beneath the surface is as important as considering the obvious variables.

This invites us to acknowledge the collaboration between our conscious and subconscious thoughts as we examine how the subconscious influences decision-making. It's admitting that your decisions are influenced by a complicated interaction between your subconscious guide's whispers and cognitive analysis. Peeling back the layers, let's continue our exploration to learn more about this complex dance in decision-making.

1. **Gut instincts and intuition:** Your subconscious can especially communicate with you when making

decisions—through gut instinct and intuition. Consider it a mild prod, utilizing all of the wisdom and insights you have amassed over the years. These imperceptible cues are vital in directing your decisions. Trusting these intuitive cues can help you make judgments that align with deeper ideas stored in your subconscious, even though they might not always come with a clear explanation.

Imagine attending a job interview and knowing that the organization might not be a good fit, even though you meet all the requirements. While your conscious mind can examine the job description and benefits, your subconscious may subtly communicate with you based on unconscious preferences or past experiences.

Consider selecting a residence. After visiting a few possibilities, one may seem to fit all the rational requirements, while another seems appropriate. That sensation, sometimes referred to as a "gut instinct," is your subconscious influencing your choice by considering elements that are not immediately apparent.

Imagine that you are meeting someone for the first time, and either you click with them right away or you sense something is wrong. Your intuition is a subconscious tool that processes nonverbal cues, memories of past interactions, and emotions to form an initial impression.

It's like drawing from a hidden wellspring of knowledge when you follow your gut. Acknowledging that your intuition might provide insightful information rather than discounting reasoned analysis is important. They are the outcome of your subconscious making sense of a tonne of data and offering a "shortcut" to making decisions.

Paying attention to your intuition can make a huge difference in everyday situations, such as selecting between two job offers or determining whether to attend a specific event. It directs you toward decisions that align with your deeper understanding, like an internal compass.

Thus, as we examine the function of gut instinct and intuition in decision-making, we must accept these imperceptible cues as important partners. It's an admission that your subconscious is an ally in helping you make decisions consistent with who you are, thanks to its abundance of gathered knowledge.

2. Emotional Factors: Let's now investigate the second factor, emotional influences. Deeply ingrained in your subconscious, emotions significantly influence how you make decisions. Emotions subtly influence your choices, whether the thrill of a fresh start, the dread of failing, or the security of comfort. Making decisions with greater balance and reason is possible when you know these underlying emotional currents.

Consider starting a new career. Even if a new opportunity offers growth and fulfillment, your decision may be influenced by your fear of leaving a stable employment. Recognizing this anxiety enables you to assess the choice with greater objectivity.

Think about purchasing a home. Practical considerations sometimes take a backseat to the joy of discovering a location that seems like home. By recognizing the emotional pull, you may compare the emotional connection to other considerations, such as location and pricing.

Now consider how comfortable routine is. When making a decision that requires you to move away from well-known routines, your subconscious feelings may oppose the change. Understanding this emotional impact allows you to determine whether following the routine is helpful or only a reaction to familiarity and comfort.

Emotional factors are similar to silent allies when it comes to making decisions. They influence your perception of possibilities and can impair your judgment. But by recognizing these feelings, you may make decisions with a greater sense of clarity about what your actual priorities and objectives are.

Consider choosing a professional route. Being conscious of these sensations enables you to make decisions that are in line with your long-term objectives rather than impulsive impulses, such as when you're feeling excited about a new task or afraid of not living up to expectations.

Emotions come into play in daily decisions, from choosing what to have for dinner to making important life decisions. Acknowledging their impact is like possessing a compass directing you across the emotional terrain, guaranteeing your choices align with your current emotions and overall goals.

Therefore, we must recognize these guiding principles when we learn more about the emotional factors that drive decision-making. It's realizing that feelings, although necessary, might occasionally take you down routes that might not align with your goals. Gaining this understanding will enable you to make choices that are in line with your short- and long-term goals. Let's investigate further, removing more layers to see how emotions maneuver through the complex domain of the subconscious.

3. Identification of Patterns: Let's now discuss the third factor, Pattern Recognition. Like a pattern investigator, your mind is skilled at identifying well-traveled routes based on prior encounters. It functions like a mental file system, allowing you to make decisions based on past experiences. Although this natural ability might make decisions easier, it's important to be conscious of potential biases and make sure that decisions take into account the particular circumstances of each case.

Think of an instance where you've interacted well with someone from a similar background. Your subconscious may help you connect with others who naturally fit that pattern by recognizing patterns in their behavior. It's important to realize, though, that this realization may inadvertently cause one to miss out on important opportunities to form relationships with others from diverse backgrounds.

Consider having to make decisions concerning your financial investments. Your subconscious may gravitate towards comparable choices if you have favorable encounters with a specific investment approach. To make sure your choice isn't based only on historical trends, it's important to strike a balance between this and a mindful awareness of the potential hazards and the state of the market now.

Consider selecting a restaurant at this point. If you've enjoyed eating at a particular restaurant, your subconscious may steer you in that direction. On the other hand, keeping an open mind about new experiences guarantees that you will take advantage of unique dining opportunities and undiscovered treasures.

Identifying patterns is like having a trustworthy helper swiftly filtering through prior encounters to provide well-traveled routes. It simplifies decision-making by referencing prior successes. However, it's critical to combine this automatic ability with deliberate thought, particularly when specific circumstances diverge from well-known patterns.

Finding patterns in daily choices, such as choosing projects or employing staff, can save time. However, being aware of such biases guarantees that choices are well-rounded and consider the particular subtleties of each circumstance. Hence, when we explore the function of pattern recognition, we must respect this innate ability and exercise caution to make judgments that are as context- and nuance-aware as feasible. Let's investigate further, removing more layers to comprehend the complex dance of decision-making in the subconscious.

4. Biases in cognition: Let's examine cognitive biases, the fourth layer, next. These operate similarly to subconsciously ingrained mental shortcuts that may inadvertently affect how you make decisions. These biases, which include availability heuristic, anchoring, and confirmation bias, affect how you process information and make decisions. It is imperative to become aware of these biases to reduce their possible impact and make more objective decisions.

Think about confirmation bias, which is the tendency for your subconscious to favor information that validates your preexisting ideas. When choosing between two possibilities, you may unconsciously ignore data that contradicts your preference and place greater weight on information that supports the option you are leaning toward.

Consider anchoring, a bias in which the first piece of information you are given unintentionally shapes your decisions. Consider negotiating a pay where the initial offer acts as an anchor that impacts your idea of a reasonable or acceptable wage range.

Now consider the availability heuristic, in which your subconscious makes decisions based on information that is easily accessible to it, frequently gleaned from recent experiences. Even if there are other good options, you could be more likely to choose a specific brand again if you've had a nice experience.

These biases are similar to unseen forces influencing how you make decisions. Being conscious of them is essential to ensuring your selections are as unbiased and well-informed as possible, even if they're natural and frequently act as effective mental shortcuts.

Consider adding a new member to the team. You may ignore important traits or abilities if you're unintentionally swayed by a single piece of information or the first impression. Being conscious of anchoring bias allows you to step back and think about the bigger picture.

Cognitive biases are present in everyday activities, from financial decisions to groceries. Gaining awareness is similar to donning glasses to improve your vision when making judgments. This enables you to avoid potential biases and make decisions that align with your preferences.

Thus, when we explore the topic of cognitive biases, it is important to recognize these imperceptible factors that affect your decision-making process. It's admitting that even while your subconscious is quite effective, it can occasionally mislead you. Your instrument for making decisions that are more objective and consistent with your true preferences is awareness. Let's continue our investigation to learn more about how the subconscious mind handles decision-making complexities.

5. Unconscious Pursuit of Goals: Let's investigate Unconscious Goal Pursuit, the sixth layer. Like a covert mission operative, your subconscious frequently pursues objectives without your conscious knowledge. This hidden work of striving subtly directs decision-making toward results consistent with underlying goals. Understanding these implicit objectives can help us better understand the motivations behind our decisions.

Consider your professional or academic decisions. Your subconscious may subtly direct you toward a particular career path due to underlying objectives like financial security or personal fulfillment. You can better match your choices with your inner ambitions by recognizing these subtle cues.

Think about your relationships. Unstated objectives in your mind could have to do with trust, friendship, or common ideals. These objectives gently direct your decisions, influencing choices that result in deep connections that satisfy your emotional requirements.

Now, consider your personal growth. Your subconscious may encourage you to develop particular traits, learn new things, or develop new abilities. Recognizing these unspoken objectives allows you to make choices that advance your ongoing development and satisfaction.

Pursuing unconscious goals is similar to having a compass pointing toward your dreams, even if you aren't aware of them. Consider deciding to pick up a new skill or pastime. Your subconscious objectives may be guiding you toward pursuits that satisfy your need for enjoyment and self-actualization.

In day-to-day living, subconscious goals influence decisions on leisure activities and habits to develop. Deciphering the hidden code that directs your decisions and identifying these goals will help you make decisions that align with your inner wants.

As we explore the idea of unconscious goal pursuit, it becomes clear that the key is recognizing your subconscious's silent architect. It's realizing that, even when conscious awareness isn't there, your mind actively pursues objectives that enhance your fulfillment and meaning in life. Increasing your understanding of this will enable you to make decisions consistent with the underlying goals that form the story of your life. Let us extend our exploration by removing further layers to comprehend the complex dance of goal pursuit in the deep domain of the subconscious.

6. Triggers for Memories: Subconscious memories can influence decisions by acting as triggers. Unconsciously, decisions might be influenced by positive or negative associations that are connected to prior experiences. Analyzing these memory triggers makes it possible to assess results and implications with greater knowledge.

Realistically speaking, it's critical to recognize how the subconscious influences judgment. Knowing these nuanced dynamics—caused by memory triggers, emotional effects, cognitive biases, pattern identification, intuition, or unconscious goal pursuit—improves one's capacity to make thoughtful judgments in various life contexts.

As we end our investigation into how the subconscious influences our ability to make decisions, we are left to navigate the unseen currents that influence our choices. The subconscious, a storehouse of feelings, desires, biases, patterns, intuition, and memories, subtly yet profoundly affects how our decisions turn out.

Recognizing the subconscious's influence on decision-making becomes useful for navigating the invisible forces at work. We reveal the complex threads that impact our decisions, from trusting our gut feelings to identifying emotional influences, being aware of cognitive biases, comprehending unconscious goal pursuit, and investigating memory triggers.

Let us leave this chapter with a heightened awareness and understanding that our subconscious plays a role in our judgments and that they are not only the result of reasoned deliberation. This insight allows us to navigate the mental undercurrents with fresh clarity and make more deliberate, thoughtful, and conscious decisions.

We carry on this self-discovery journey with every choice we make, revealing the factors that mold our course by removing the layers of the subconscious. Anticipate more insights into the subtle arrangements within the maze of the human mind in the upcoming chapter. May the knowledge acquired here clear the path and enable us to make choices with discernment, awareness, and a stronger sense of the subtle currents inside.

---

11 Hidden Influential Powers

Unleashing The Unseen Forces That Shape Success And Leadership

HALBERT WARD

INTRODUCTION

If you are asked to talk about what you think your perfect day should look like? What would it be?

Would you be spending the entire day playing with your children? Do you imagine yourself sitting on a bench next to a lake and drinking your favorite beer? Or do you imagine yourself signing that big cheque?

Most people want to be successful and obsess over how to achieve the success they desire because everyone wants to feel like they matter.

Success means different things to different people. So, how do you define your success? Is it defined by marrying the most beautiful girl or the hottest guy in the country, getting a big paycheck, living in a luxurious home, or driving the most expensive car in your neighborhood?

Those things are not the true measure of success. Becoming successful is not about frivolous things. A love for your career and unique talents are required to build a business. You need the ability and opportunity to uncover your dream.

First, you need to sit down and imagine where you see yourself in the next five years. Whether you become successful or not is up to you.

So, are you ready to figure out what to do to be successful and influential and then start doing it? Or do you want to be left alone to continue dreaming about it?

If you are serious about becoming a successful and influential person and don't want to be sitting on a couch, watching TV, and still dreaming in the next five years, keep reading.

What is something that is commonly found in every successful individual? Is it good looks, intelligence, hard work, or the ability to never give up? The answer is relationships.

Behind every successful individual, you will find a network of people who provide the appropriate support to that individual at the right time. You need to understand that no individual has ever accomplished anything alone.

Successful people have a legion of other great minds who are contributing engineering skills and intellectual capital. They may have a community that nurtured them and protected them on their journey. They may also have the inspiration of their parents and a manufacturer who decided to help them produce their products. Even accomplishments that appear to be achievements made by individuals alone are backed by a lifetime of relationships that helped that individual to succeed.

It appears that the more influential and established a person's network is, the greater the individual's ability to lead others, solve problems, provide ideas, and accomplish something great.

No exceptions exist. Professional and personal success is connected to building relationships, and it will continue to be this way.

Sadly, people who think networking is all about handing out business cards or trying to convince clients at business functions have tagged the term "networking" negative.

The reality is that great networking involves creating relationships, building them, and maintaining them. Some individuals make their living helping other people to build successful relationships. These individuals can successfully help people to build stronger business relationships. Formulaic activities or rehearsed statements are not what effective networking is about. Rather it is about making people know, trust, and like us.

So, are you ready to finally discover how to achieve success in your personal and professional life?

If you want to be successful and influential, there are unseen forces that shape success and leadership. The eleven chapters of this book discuss them. After reading this book, you will learn to harness the hidden influential powers within you.

To become successful as a leader and use your power to influence others positively, you need to first understand all about powers in leadership. So, let us start by discussing the powers that effective leaders use.

CHAPTER 1
Understanding Powers In Leadership

Many leaders have allowed power to go to their heads. These leaders believe that their position gives them the authority to rule the people with an iron fist. In the short term, they might succeed in getting the people to do their will by imposing it on them. But in the long term, this management style can be bad for business as it can lead to lower employee engagement.

A great leader has a perfect understanding of the different types of power and also understands how to combine them with influence tactics. They are aware that they can achieve great results this way.

But what exactly is power?

We will discuss what power is and look at the different types of power that effective leaders use. We will also take a look at how the different types of power can be used to lead more effectively.

Power is possessing the ability or capacity to impose your will on other people or act in certain ways. In the context of work, the concept of power is often interpreted in different ways by different individuals.

Some individuals see power as something they get from an external source. This power could be a position or title that is assigned to someone and gives them authority and control over others.

Other individuals believe that power, which is an innate quality, manifests externally and can be cultivated internally. The personal power of an individual grows as they develop.

True power combines internal power as well as external power. This means that any individual can access a certain amount of power, no matter what their position in the hierarchy is.

Power is the capacity to act or the ability to impose one's will on other people. In the context of work, there are different ways that the concept of power is interpreted.

Some individuals get external power from the positions or titles they are assigned, while other individuals believe that people can develop it internally and manifest it externally. Leaders who are the most effective influence others with the use of their power and their external power.

Leadership power is a leader's ability and influence that they possess to guide, direct, and motivate other individuals toward achieving a common goal. It encompasses a leader's authority and control over their organization or team. Leadership power involves the leader's capacity to allocate resources, make decisions, and shape the direction of individuals or a group. This power is not only based on the title or position that a leader has, but it is also based on the leader's skills, personal qualities, and the trust and respect that their followers give them. When a leader is effective, it means that the leader uses communication, influence, and persuasion to empower and inspire other individuals to achieve shared objectives.

Influence and Power

Powerful leaders have the capability to influence others. A combination of the innate leadership qualities that the leaders possess and the way other people perceive them is what their power is based on.

However, when you have power, it doesn't necessarily mean that you will have influence. The leaders who are the most powerful uplift their members and support them instead of controlling and dominating them. Servant leaders have the greatest influence as they put their employees' needs and development first.

Leaders who are the most powerful have self-discipline and clarity. This makes them lead people by example.

When the leaders model disciplined behaviors, their team members are also encouraged to do the same. Self-disciplined employees require less micro-management. The leader's power is then increased, and a virtuous cycle of trust is created as well as self-leadership.

Another major aspect of power that a leader has is insightfulness. An insightful leader can see the bigger picture and they are also able to communicate that vision. The insights that the leader has given them greater influence and power over the members of their team.

A leader will be seen as more powerful by their employees when they have a greater impact. Your perceived power can be increased among your employees when you use your creativity to make decisions, set organizational goals, and find solutions.

Leaders who are confident also have more influence and power over their subordinates. Confidence can be cultivated by defending your positions and acting in accordance with your values.

Types of Power

Before we discuss the different bases of power, it is important to know that the bases of power are not all equally effective. Some types of power are capable of making your employees comply with the demands you have, but they won't win the support of the employees. Sometimes, these types of power can be helpful in moments when an employee should be disciplined.

There are other types of power that are more influential. With them, you gain your employees' commitment and support, and this makes your organization have better outcomes.

When you understand the different types of power, you will be aware of which of the different types of power will most likely bring about positive results. You will be aware of which power bases you should not depend too much on.

Depending on the particular situation, a great leader has an understanding of how to use the different types of power.

Studies show that managers in the workplace have greater influence over burnout and employee well-being than working hours.

It is important that you are wise with the use of your power as a leader since a large percentage of employees burn out at some point. If you don't use your power wisely, you will contribute to employee disengagement and reduce the productivity of your team and they will be more likely to quit working. Unwise use can even cause burnout.

Leaders use power to motivate their teams and drive them to success. It can be used to inspire commitment, build relationships, and accomplish results. Becoming a more effective leader requires that you have an understanding of the five types of power, the effectiveness of each one, and the appropriate time to use them.

The following are the five main types of power and the real-world benefits that each of them offers:

The legitimate type of power

Legitimate power, which is also referred to as positional power, is the authority and influence that an individual gets from their role or formal position in a social structure or organization. This is based on the belief that people who are in certain positions have the right to make decisions that impact others, and they can also exert control. Society or the organization typically grants legitimate power, and this power is acknowledged and accepted by the people who are being influenced.

You receive this type of power when you occupy a particular position in your company. It is a formal power that grants authority and control over others. Leaders should make wise use of their power as there can be employee disengagement and burnout if leaders don't use their power wisely.

This power gives you authority within the company, and it depends on the particular position you occupy. As long as you remain in that position, you have that power. Subordinates recognize this type of power. As a result of this, the power works well in hierarchical organizations, such as the military.

You can obtain this legitimate power by showing that you possess the skills that the role requires.

This power can be taken away since it was given to you. So, you must ensure that you don't abuse it.

Effective leaders are not solely dependent on legitimate power. Instead, they use the power in combination with other types of power.

Legitimate power is usually considered the most effective; however, it is dependent on the individual who is the leader possessing the right kind of power that motivates their team. Although this power involves the authority that is given to a leader based on the position or title that they have, you need to know that the power can also have negative consequences and may not always be as successful as people may think. The best way to use legitimate power is when it is combined with other types of power.

Legitimate power is present in different settings, such as in educational institutions, the workplace, within social groups, and in government. The power that a teacher possesses to establish rules and regulations and guide students, a manager's power to evaluate employees and assign tasks, or a political leader's power to make decisions for their constituents are examples of legitimate power.

The formal authority that is linked with the role or position is where this legitimate power is derived from, and it is usually backed by policies, rules, and organizational structures. However, the ability of the leader to use legitimate power respectably and fairly and the individuals' willingness to recognize and accept their authority is what the effectiveness of legitimate power depends on.

The referent type of power

Referent power is the type of power that provides a leader with the greatest level of influence.

This power is based on an individual's relationships and attributes. It is usually connected to an individual's confidence, charisma, and likability. When a person has strong personal relationships, they are able to influence others in ways that individuals who lack strong personal relationships cannot.

Qualities that inspire respect and trust in their co-workers are where leaders get referent power from. Integrity and honesty are some of these qualities. An individual with referent power exudes confidence and possesses excellent interpersonal skills. As a result of this, these leaders are natural leaders who listen to their colleagues and also support and help them.

Referent power is not external but internal. It cannot be transferred to you from someone else because it is a personal power. Your ability to influence your colleagues grows as your referent power grows.

This type of power is the most influential. It is obtained through qualities such as excellent interpersonal skills, honesty, and integrity. It cannot be given to another individual as it is a personal power that is internal. If referent power is used in the right way, it can motivate the people around the leader and it is less confrontational than the other types of power. A leader's capacity to influence their colleagues increases as their referent power grows.

This type of power is based on the respect, admiration, and identification that other people have towards a person. It comes from the person's personal characteristics, charisma, and qualities, rather than the person's authority or formal position. Referent power is usually associated with people who are considered influential figures, mentors, or role models within an organization or a group.

Individuals who possess referent power have qualities that other individuals aspire to emulate or that others find desirable. A sense of trust and admiration is created among their followers by their attributes, such as their communication skills, expertise, integrity, empathy, or charisma. For this reason, people are more willing to listen to individuals with referent power and be influenced by them.

Referent power doesn't come from control or formal authority, but it comes from the strength of the relationship that exists between the influential individual and their followers. This power is built on the perception that the individual has a genuine concern about the success and the well-being of others and is also built on trust and mutual respect.

This power is one of the most valuable powers that is available. It involves the way you build relationships and develop them. Referent power is reliant on personal values and traits, such as trustworthiness, integrity, and honesty. Individuals who have referent power can highly influence any individual who respects and admires them.

Leaders with referent power usually impact their organization or team positively. They can inspire others and motivate them, encourage cooperation and collaboration, and promote a sense of commitment and loyalty. They gain influence from their ability to connect with other individuals on an emotional level and win their support through their behaviors and personal qualities.

You need to understand that referent power is based on other people's perceptions and subjective judgment. Different individuals may have different sources of admiration or role models. Therefore, leaders need to cultivate their positive qualities and behaviors and consistently maintain them to keep their referent power and the influence that they have.

The reward type of power

Reward power involves possessing the capacity to provide benefits or rewards to motivate other individuals. Benefits or rewards are offered in exchange for achieving a result or performing a task.

Rewards are often provided in the form of benefits, public praise, salary raises, or promotions. When reward power is used strategically, it can bring about intrinsic motivation among employees and also motivate the employees to produce more. For rewards to be effective, they have to be tangible and meaningful to employees.

Reward power is not often as effective as some people who are leaders think it is. Individuals who can motivate people to respond to win awards, promotions, and raises are those who hold this power. For instance, managers possess a certain amount of reward power if they give their subordinates performance reviews that determine whether they get bonuses and raises.

The power should be tangible enough and relevant to give your employees motivation. It should not depend on your superiors and should also be something that you can give because it is within your power. Results can be achieved with this type of power, but that doesn't mean that the commitment and support of your employees are ensured.

Reward power is based on the idea that people are motivated by the promise of benefits or positive outcomes. It is also believed that the people who distribute or control these rewards have the ability to influence other people's actions and behaviors. So, this power is a type of influence that comes from an individual's ability to provide incentives or rewards to other individuals.

Individuals who possess reward power have control or authority over recognition, benefits, resources, promotions, or any other valuable outcomes that people desire. They use these rewards to reinforce certain performances from other individuals and also to encourage and motivate them.

We can see reward power in various settings, such as in personal relationships, education, and the workplace. For instance, a manager with the power to give promotions, bonuses, or salary raises can drive the performance and productivity of employees by using these rewards as incentives. In the same way, a teacher who offers praise or rewards for exemplary behavior or good grades can influence students to work towards achieving excellence.

People with reward power need to use it fairly and responsibly, ensuring that they distribute rewards based on performance, merit, or some other objective criteria. When reward power is used effectively, it can create a motivating and positive environment, encourage behaviors that are desired, and also enhance engagement and job satisfaction.

However, it is important to know that over-dependence on reward power without looking at the importance of meaningful work or other types of motivation such as intrinsic motivation, may bring about reliance on external rewards as well as potential decreases in intrinsic motivation. Leaders should work to create a balance between making appropriate use of rewards and promoting a sense of intrinsic motivation as well as fulfillment among their followers.

The expert type of power

Expert power is the power that one gets from having expertise and knowledge in a specific area at high levels. You have this type of power when you have both extensive experience in the area of your expertise and deep technical knowledge. This power is obtained through experience and knowledge which gives the leader respect and credibility before the individuals in the workplace. Leaders with expert power can influence their co-workers at every level in the organization. These leaders are also able to lead both the individual's development and the company's development. However, a leader who possesses expert power knows how important it is to constantly develop their skills and knowledge to stay credible.

The individual with this power is given the ability to teach and influence other individuals. When teaching or leading a team, expert power can help an individual develop respect and trust.

People in your workplace will be naturally drawn to you if you are an expert in your field. They will come to you to gain benefit from the knowledge you have. You get credibility from your expertise, and people respect and trust your opinions. You gain the ability to influence your colleagues across the different levels of the company with your expert power. It makes you able to help with the growth and development of your co-workers and the entire organization.

However, an individual who is a true expert is aware that they must continue developing their skills and knowledge to maintain their credibility.

Expert power comes from the top-level skills you have as well as your years of experience. Your peers will see you as an influential person once you have expert knowledge. If an individual holds an MBA and a PhD in a particular field, their colleagues will respect them for their expertise. This makes them influential in that field.

This power is based on the belief that people who have expertise or specialized knowledge are trustworthy and credible sources of guidance and information. Since this type of power is a form of influence that originates from an individual's skills, knowledge, and expertise in a specific area, individuals with expert power are considered competent, and their recommendations and opinions are respected and influence other people.

Expert power is present in various contexts, such as the school, the workplace, or any situation where people have unique skills or knowledge. For instance, a professor in the university who is an expert in a particular field can influence their students' perspectives and understanding with their expert power. In the same way, a professional who is highly skilled in a particular industry can use their expert power to guide individuals and inform decision-making within the company.

For expert power to be established, people need to show that they have a deep understanding and mastery of their field, which can be demonstrated through experience, education, certifications, or achievements that are noteworthy. Experts need to continuously stay abreast of new developments in their specific field and update their knowledge to maintain their credibility.

Leaders who have expert power can effectively influence other individuals by providing valuable insights, sharing their expertise, and providing solutions to complex problems. People usually look for these leaders to obtain guidance and they help in shaping decisions and opinions. However, it is important for people with expert power to use their influence ethically and responsibly, ensuring that their expertise is used in ways that are helpful for growth and development.

Nobody can take this power from you. Your knowledge gives you this power. However, you need to keep learning new things and improving to remain an expert.

The coercive type of power

Coercive power is the least effective and is commonly used in many workplaces. Leaders are advised to not use coercive power. This power involves forcing people to do your will by using threats. They do what they have to do because they are afraid of repercussions like losing their jobs, even though they might not agree with what they have to do.

For instance, in many organizations, leaders ask for constant new ideas and innovation from their employees. Employees who don't measure up might be replaced by another individual.

Although coercive power may be effective in the short term, it creates disengaged, unhappy employees and it is best to avoid it. Employee retention efforts can also be negatively affected by it.

Coercive power involves using punishment or fear to influence others. Coercive power is the least effective since it is capable of resulting in resistance and mistrust from employees. You need to understand the types of power if you want to be an effective leader. You also need to be aware of how each of the power works and the best time to use them.

No space or time really exists for coercive power in the workplace. Fear cannot win loyalty and respect from your employees now or even in the long run. No matter how good you are as a leader, fear likely won't win. Using coercive power in the workplace is just like bullying, and you cannot build credibility with it.

Coercive power is based on punishing or making threats to make other people do as one desires, even if these people are not in agreement. Coercive power is used by leaders to push for new ideas or innovation. Sadly, coercive power usually creates an environment of mistrust and fear and this could result in alienation and employee resentment.

Since this power is a type of influence that is reliant upon the ability to impose punishments or negative consequences on others to gain obedience or compliance, it stands on the idea that the threat of punishment or fear can influence people.

Individuals who have coercive power have the capacity or authority to enforce disciplinary actions, rules, and regulations. These individuals can compel other people to behave in a certain way or deter undesirable behavior by using penalties, punishments, or other forms of negative reinforcement.

Although coercive power can be helpful when it comes to achieving immediate compliance, it usually results in negative consequences in the long term. It can lead to resentment, fear, and low morale among people who feel oppressed or coerced. And this is capable of undermining creativity, motivation, and trust within the group that is affected.

Individuals and leaders who depend heavily on coercive power may experience challenges when it comes to developing relationships that are positive and promote collaboration. Effectiveness is higher when you employ other forms of power, such as referent power, expert power, or legitimate power, which focuses on inspiring other people and motivating them rather than depending on punishment or fear.

Using the Different Types of Power

Power in leadership is important as it helps teams get to greater performance levels. Anyone in a managerial position will discover that the ability to motivate and lead others is valuable as it will inspire their teams to accomplish great things.

Powerful leaders are usually very persuasive. Power is usually seen as something that is connected to influence and credibility. You capture people's hearts and minds and they are moved to take action when you are influencing others.

Many people have power but don't know what to do with it. Some people allow power to get to their heads because they don't know how to handle it well. For this reason, you must understand the different types of power and know what type of power you are using.

Effective leaders are aware of how to use the different types of power that exist whenever they find themselves in any situation. They can use them in different situations. They usually develop this skill with experience.

Understand that some types of power will only be effective when the situations require immediate resolution or action.

When an employee's misconduct is involved, coercion might be used to persuade your worker to stop displaying inappropriate behavior. Your discretion should be used to determine if you are doing the right thing.

You will often be reliant on softer types of power to help encourage your employees to be committed to the goals and plans of the organization. These include referent, legitimate, and expert power.

A powerful leader is aware of how to appropriately use each source of power whenever the need arises. Before you apply each type of power, you must understand them. Once you understand each of the types of power, you can come up with ways to use them at work.

The following are some tips on how an individual can effectively use the different types of power:

Know the end goal: When you clearly understand the end goal, it becomes easier to plan and you are also able to use the different types of power in appropriate ways. It can be easier for you to come up with a plan when you understand your goal. We can say the same for leadership styles as well as types of power. Before motivating your team or delegating work, you need to understand what you want to accomplish.

Know your team: There is a need for you to know your team well by having casual coffee chats, one-on-one meetings, and check-ins. Knowing the person you are speaking to and what they find valuable is important. Casual coffee chats, one-on-one meetings, or employee engagement surveys that are more structured can help you know your team members better. You will know which power types to use and when to use them when you make yourself familiar with your team.

Work on your leadership style: Various types of power are supported by different leadership styles, so ensure that you completely understand each of the types of power before applying them. What is your leadership style like? Are you a democratic leader? Do you usually like to hear from each person before making any decision? Or are you the type of individual who takes a more top-down approach? Various types of power are supported by different leadership styles, so for great leadership, try to see them as a cohesive partnership.

Try a different approach: When you are using various types of power, you need to stay flexible and be willing to receive feedback. You can try another approach if yours is not working the way you expect it to. The first time you use a new type of power, you might achieve great success. But if it does not resonate with your own values or your team, or if it falls flat, you can try a different approach. When you are flexible and remain open to feedback, the process will be made easier.

You can get greater influence, boost the engagement of the employees in your organization, and get better results with the different types of power.

Understanding the best way to use your power is a skill that experience and time usually bring. However, the process can be accelerated and you can become a more influential leader with a coach's support and in less time as well.

Leveraging Influence and Power to Achieve Success

Influence and power are two different concepts that can make a positive and powerful difference in an organization when they are used appropriately. A leader gets power from their position, whereas they get influence from the relationships they have developed, as well as their persuasion and communication skills. It is crucial to use influence to connect and to exercise power judiciously.

Great leaders are aware of how to use power and influence appropriately and they know how to leverage both to achieve success. Once you fully understand the difference between power and influence and you master both, you will become better at your craft. For this process to be accelerated, leaders need to consider getting a coach who has the ability to coach them and help them use their influence and power effectively.

A person's ability to influence people effectively lies in the establishment of trust between the individual who is the influencer and the subjects. It can be achieved through an understanding of the concerns and needs of the people, meaningful conversations, and joint problem-solving. Being aware of the motivations and interests of the people you are trying to influence is important to achieve the highest level of effectiveness.

You can leverage power and influence to create a successful leadership legacy. Influence guides inspiration and example, while power should be used to make decisions. It can be challenging to use both power and influence effectively to become a respected and admired leader, but it can be achieved with the help of a coach who can teach you how to apply them properly.

The following tips will help you maximize influence and power:

Know the difference that exists between influence and power.

Power is based on an individual's role or title in the organization.

An individual gains influence through the relationships they develop with other individuals.

Use the power you have constructively and positively to gain trust and respect.

Listen to the concerns and needs of the people you are influencing and completely understand their concerns and needs.

Understand the people's motivations and interests to achieve better influence.

Seek out a mentor or coach to learn how to use influence and power effectively.

Leadership Power and the Workplace

Leaders can motivate their employees and increase productivity in the workplace if they use their power correctly. They can promote self-discipline, set high expectations, and promote coordination among different departments. However, the abuse or misuse of these powers can result in inefficiency, low morale, and high staff turnover. Leaders who are effective know how important it is to balance their powers and use them appropriately to create a positive and productive environment in the workplace.

The continuous hustle as well as the change in the business world today requires that leaders are also digital pioneers. And you are at the center of a big transformation since you are a leader. Today, the boss doesn't just hand out tasks from their office and then keep the employees in check through the use of their coercive power. This used to happen more in the past than now. Now, the leader of an organization is similar to being the captain of a ship. The leader has to navigate uncharted digital waters every day, as they coordinate services and processes online, and ensure that remote team members are working together and are being productive.

Your leadership style is the only map. Your leadership skills and social power are what your ability to keep the rudder of your ship on course and continue moving your organization forward toward a future that is built on adaptability, innovation, and profitable growth depends largely on.

Today's power is not contained in the inherent authority that your title carries or in the prestige of your position. It is nuanced. Today, employees have given up offices to work from remote home offices and there is an increase in the number of customers who are demanding services and purchasing goods from the comfort of their home. It is important that you understand the types of leadership power as well as how to apply these types of leadership power to motivate, influence, and lead your team. This is important for your success.

Social psychologists have identified five different bases of power, which are categorized into personal and formal powers. Each type of power is distinct when it comes to leading and, also getting people to do the job.

Important insights are provided by these five bases of social power, and they are still very relevant as they can be used to refine your style of leadership and successfully navigate these uncertain times. We will take a closer look at these powers in the context of formal and personal power.

Enhancing Leadership with Formal Power

Formal power is power that originates directly from the role you play in the organization. It's connected to the title you have and the authority that comes with the title, and as part of your leadership toolkit, different types are available that you can tap into.

Legitimate power

This power stems from the official position you have in the organization. You have this power because you are in charge. The authority to set direction, make decisions, and ask your team to follow you is yours.

Legitimate power gives you the authority to guide your team and make decisions, but when you involve your team in the decision-making process, it helps to instill a sense of ownership, and build trust, and it also results in better outcomes for everybody. Promoting collaboration and open communication is important.

Reward power

Reward power involves recognizing and rewarding the accomplishments of your team whether they are big or small accomplishments.

If you have an employee who has been consistent with doing their job and outperforming on their goals, you can give them a public shout-out, offer them a shout-out during a virtual team meeting, or you can motivate the whole team and not just the person. Reward power can bring about a positive work environment that promotes productivity and increases job satisfaction if it is done right.

Coercive power

Coercive power originates from possessing the ability to create negative consequences for your team or punish them. For instance, when you issue a warning to your project manager that they will be sacked if their team fails to meet an important project milestone, you are using coercive power.

While this type of power can work in the short term, it can result in significant issues like higher turnover or lower morale if you rely on it too much. This power should only be used sparingly, to ensure that standards are met, not to instill fear in people.

Building Trust and Respect with Personal Power

Personal power has to do with you. It involves your charisma, knowledge, and personality. It is not about your role or title. You can enhance your leadership and drive success with these two types of personal power.

Referent power

Referent power can be said to be the most enduring of all the types of power available. This is when your team identifies with you and respects you on a personal level. Maybe people know you for how you always control yourself under pressure, for your ability to show empathy, or for your integrity. Referent power helps to build relationships that are strong and trust-based, and you will find that it is invaluable today as face-to-face interactions are becoming limited with connections becoming more important in today's remote work environment.

By allowing your personality to shine, even if it is through a computer screen, you are able to promote a culture of authenticity and respect.

Expert power

Expert power stems from what you are aware of. It is your expertise, knowledge, or unique skills in a specific area. You may have a knack for market trends or you may be an analytics expert. This power gives you influence and respect because you bring value to the table.

When expert power is involved, your team listens to you and respects you because you have expert knowledge of what you are talking to them about. For instance, when you break down strategic initiatives or share insights that have to do with market trends during a team meeting, your expert power is at work.

You need to be a lifelong learner to maintain your expert power. When you continue keeping up with the latest trends, you will stay on your game with the knowledge you will gain in your field.

Striking a Balance Between Personal and Formal Power in Leadership

During this period when change is accelerated and remote work is increasing in popularity, both personal and formal powers are important. However, there is a change in the way personal and formal power influence teams.

Reward, coercive, and legitimate power are types of formal power that are necessary and relevant. They help the organization to move forward toward its goals. And the authority is needed to help you set direction, make decisions, enforce standards, and distribute rewards.

Still, when you have a certain role or title, it is not enough to successfully move your organization forward or lead your team. Team members like to feel valued, respected, and heard. So, while you are given the chance to make the decisions with formal power, you will have more accomplishment and innovation by allowing your team to provide feedback and by allowing collaboration.

Ultimately, when you leverage your formal power, it takes a transparent and fair approach to penalties and rewards and it also takes balance. Your team does not feel threatened but they feel motivated as that kind of authentic use of formal power ensures that.

Referent and expert power, which are the personal power types, are getting more critical. Your team in the organization looks to you for inspiration and expertise and not just for directives and assignments. You have to be ready to share ideas and insights that can keep your business moving ahead. Your personal traits, which include your resilience, empathy, and integrity, will help you and your team to connect on a deeper level. This is important in a remote work scenario, where it can be challenging to build trust and rapport but is absolutely important.

In today's world, the leadership journey is a nuanced one. It is a balance between empathy and authority, between instilling discipline and offering rewards, and between setting direction and cultivating collaboration.

When people see you as a powerful person, they will rely on you, and this is a natural thing. You can achieve a lot with that influence. These different types of power have advantages and disadvantages.

Being a business leader, your role evolves, and your team continues to look to you for motivation and guidance. You have the power to boost morale, drive results, inspire innovation, and create a culture where the members of your team are productive, motivated, and desire to remain at the company. So, success lies in striking the right balance, whether you are using your personal power to lead and inspire your team or you are using your formal power to guide your team. You will be able to lead your organization toward success with the balance.

CHAPTER 2
Understanding Influencers

One of the greatest undertakings of a leader is influencing people. Influence is the ability to have an effect on the behavior, development, and character of an individual or something.

When you are someone who has that kind of effect on other individuals, it means that you have power. This power is not a power that comes from coercion; instead, it is a strength that comes from within you and causes people to pay attention to you and listen to what you have to say to them. It makes them want to work with you and share your vision.

What makes you an influential figure in your workplace? There are certain traits that influential people have. People think about those that influence them most nearly every day as they make decisions.

Is there someone in your life who is intentional about knowing the names of everyone that they work with and also sends hand-written cards or something memorable to these colleagues on their birthdays and other special occasions?

Is this person transparent and always ready to see that a project is properly done? You may know someone like this who wants the best for everybody around them. You know that they have a positive influence on your work ethic and you even wish to be like them because they are your cheerleader.

They have taught you a lot of things and they reach out to celebrate milestones you have reached and important events. They also reach out when you are experiencing grief.

There may also be someone who influences you but you have never met them personally. You just feel like you know them intimately through their daily meditations, novels, and memoirs.

The deep love they have for humanity and the boldness with which they speak out in any setting get you motivated to speak with confidence. Whenever you read the books they have written, you strive to be more like them.

You may have noticed that as you think about the influential figures in your life, they have the qualities you desire to have in yourself. When you have decided to become an influential person, following the steps of your influencers is a great place to start. This will help you chart your own course.

Characteristics of Influencers

Social media may have introduced you to influencers. However, that type of influence does not have much in common with effective influence in the workplace. Once you have a full understanding of what it feels like to be inspired by individuals who have left a mark on your life, you know what it means for someone to have a meaningful influence.

The following characteristics show that someone is a person of influence:

Influencers are intentional

You can spot an individual who is deliberate by how willing and ready they are to take action in their work as well as their lives. This individual knows their priorities and uses efficient scheduling to prioritize things to be done throughout the day while paying attention to the long-term view. They are careful with choosing their words because they understand that words matter when it comes to influencing.

They use research and collaboration with other people to get ready for their presentations so that they can deliver their best in any particular situation. And this person is consistent with this as they practice these behaviors regularly and follow a daily routine.

Influencers connect

When you find yourself in the space of an individual who is influential, they include you. Sometimes, they ask you questions, and they may even offer you feedback at other times. They do this to bring you into the circle of trust.

You are reminded by this connection that the individual does not choose to do it alone, even though they are leading the effort. This is what makes you much more likely to desire to collaborate with them as you are happy about the possibilities of the things you might accomplish together with them.

Influencers are resilient

The person who is influential knows that things may not always go as planned. So, they are always ready to look for new ways to manage a situation when the unexpected happens. This new strategy is something they are also willing to share with their team.

By revealing what they are experiencing and taking calculated risks, you are aware that they will be there for the long haul. The challenges offer the individual who is influential a chance to reframe and come up with a new plan to follow. They are not afraid of challenges.

Influencers are continuous learners

When you find yourself in the influential person's presence, you are aware that this person is a step ahead because of their ability to grow and learn constantly. They never announce to you that they have arrived, because they are aware that something around the corner will interest them.

It is this particular passion that you have for growth that makes you read an important book about your business, stay up late to study, or take that course.

If you want to build influence, the following steps will help you change how you relate to your superiors, colleagues, or any individual in your life:

Maintain integrity

You are aligned with yourself and coherent when the actions you take come from a core value of integrity. An individual who has integrity is complete and whole. When you act with integrity, you carry yourself with you at home, work, or wherever you are. You are aware that what you do impacts the people around you.

Also, you are the same individual. And regardless of the setting, you are recognizable. Integrity means coherence between your words, actions, and values, no matter the context.

Ensure that you do the thing you say you will do. If you set a goal that involves getting other people to count on you, ensure that you do your best to honor the commitments you have made. When you tell someone that you will give them a response by 11 am the next day, do your best to send the response before that time. If anything stops you from doing that, let someone know that you are working on it and let them know when you will send the response. You become a reliable person when other people see that you are dependable.

Ensure that people are heard and understood

Even though you would like to share the ideas you have, pause before you speak and allow another individual to share or introduce a suggestion. When you ensure that the people who are around you are heard and understood, they feel free to say what they want to say. Others are empowered by you when you offer them this opportunity, and they don't feel excluded from the process. They feel included in it.

Be a good listener

Being a good listener involves your state of mind. When you pay attention and listen to what someone is saying, you are present. Instead of paying attention to what you want to say, pay attention to what the other person is saying. In fact, you can listen to what they have said and practice a part of the sentence or the last sentence that the person says. When you repeat what they are saying, the person feels heard and you form a connection with them because they are aware that you are listening to them. You can also choose to paraphrase what they have said. You can say something like, "I heard you say that you will...." This will help you understand what they are saying and then show that you care enough to understand what they are saying. Then you can request clarification immediately if you are confused about anything they have said. People don't usually like to listen. So, listening genuinely can help you increase your influence with the individual you are listening to.

Focus on relevant issues

When you separate yourself from irrelevant issues and unnecessary competition, it makes you stand out as an influential person. This happens because you are focused on knowing what unique qualities others have so they can perform more productively. You take strategic steps, lead your team to the next level, and demonstrate exceptional standards in your work.

Check your wellbeing

Check-in with yourself regularly in order to stay present so that other individuals can follow as you lead the way. This involves checking your emotional, physical, and spiritual well-being. Check if you are eating and exercising well and regulating your emotions. When you need to talk, who are the individuals you turn to? Do you spend time to reflect or be mindful? You will be more likely to pay attention to the needs of the people around you when your needs are being met.

Show interest

One great way to make people show interest in your project and get them to join you is by being interested in your project. Authentic excitement and passion are contagious, and this happens especially when the impact is clear.

Getting influence through conviction and example will not get you millions of followers. But in the office, it can have a ripple effect that is longer-lasting, shaping organizational decisions, culture, and direction, and earning loyalty and commitment.

As you grow influence, you may not know that you are making an impact on someone else with what you are doing. You might give feedback, be thorough, support a colleague, or complete a project that you find challenging because that is who you are and what you do. Your character forms when nobody is watching.

Connect with others

If you want individuals to show interest in your destination, you need to do the things that will make them connect with you in a meaningful and authentic way. You know the tendencies and names of the individuals you work with on every level and you also look for ways to make them give their best. You face challenges as a group and you also celebrate your successes together. People around you will find you to be transparent when they feel like they know you very well.

Stay relevant

When you are influential, it means that you are up to date with your industry's latest developments. You are set to pivot, and when the time to make changes has come. You are aware of the change as well and you welcome the constant change.

If you want to influence in the workplace today, you should not be holding fast to the "I know best" or the "way things are done" cliché. Observing forecasts and trends, you adapt to the situation and reinforce the particular things you know and the things you need to know. You are aware of practices that can strengthen your business and make it more competitive.

CHAPTER 3
Influence: The Key To Success

Success starts with your personal influence level. In the past few years, influence has become a major buzzword.

Major organizations are investing a lot of money to build the skills, confidence, and morale of employees. They hold team-building retreats, workshops, and conferences in different parts of the world. These organizations do this intending to increase their influence. This may be working, but it could work faster. They can also get long-lasting results.

Another way to increase your morale and confidence as well as your productivity and profits is to increase your influence potential.

Successful companies know that employees as well as teams are most productive when they influence other people effectively. They invest in the company's employees and they nurture the company's human capital both emotionally and intellectually by providing the tools they require to maximize their influence potential.

When teams, managers, and executives influence effectively, employee productivity is maximized. The major key to unlocking the presence, position, and performance of the company is influence. When individuals influence their teams, themselves, and each other, they have a formula for success that is unimaginable.

And it begins with the personal influence you have, which is being influential. The most significant capability you have to achieve success in your company, business, and personal life is your personal influence. It all begins with sowing the seeds of presence and influential behavior. In all that you do, starting at the beginning will always give you the best results.

What can you do to become influential? True influence is not just shaking a person's hands in a particular way, making eye contact, or creating a stance of reciprocity. It is deeper than all that, and it doesn't happen overnight. It starts from inside of you and moves outward.

Impacting people is what influence is about. A direct correlation exists between your personal influence and your impact on all of the interactions you have. Being an influential person makes you have more influence. Things become easier to get done the more you influence people. Whether you are putting yourself in line to get promoted, leading change in your organization, or trying to get big sales, your influence can determine or have a big impact on how successful you will be.

Being influential means that you have a presence that nobody can deny. You just have to show up and nobody can deny the presence. Influence is a valuable thing you have, and it can help you accomplish great things in life. So, you need to stop stressing yourself looking for ways to get more of what you want in life when using your influence can make things easier for you.

Using Influence Constructively

Although every one of us strives to be successful, we think about success in different ways. Many stereotypical views of success exist and they may sometimes prevent people from realizing that they have already achieved success.

When you understand what is required and you use your influence in a positive way, success comes. Leaders are aware that what makes them successful is not the control they have over other individuals, but they understand that what makes them successful is their ability to positively influence other individuals to develop as human beings and accomplish goals.

The following tips should be considered if you want to achieve the kind of success that allows you to be a positive influence:

Listen to learn during conversations

When you allow yourself to listen, you ensure that you are truly present while the conversation is going on and you are able to listen to learn. When you listen to learn, it enhances your empathy, objectivity, and ability to accept that not everybody has the same perceptions or opinions as us. This way, you create an environment and the opportunity for everybody to learn and grow. This can be hard if the individual you are having a conversation with doesn't want to slow down or is not listening to learn. However, you can show them the way with your positive influence. If necessary, you can ask them if they can continue the conversation at another time. Ensure that you do this without completely dismissing the points they have. Leadership involves slowing down when someone is talking and listening to learn.

When you focus on yourself and do your best, other individuals will be influenced as they watch you lead by example.

Learn effective delegation

Effective delegation is important when it comes to managing and leading teams in an organization. There is a careful selection process, and during this process, the right person to handle the task is assigned the delegated task. Identifying the right person for the task requires recognizing the individual with the skills that the task requires or the individual who is willing to learn about that task and complete it. Team members may become disconnected from the common goal if the delegation process is not handled mindfully. If the message is not properly communicated to the right person, the meaning becomes lost.

Be honest

If you find yourself in conversations in which the other individual is not slowing down to pay attention to the situation or if they are not listening to learn, your honesty about their inattention can get them back on track. Honesty can bring them back to the present and they will pursue the common goal. Also, honesty will help greatly in your influence because it makes people trust you to tell them the truth.

Slow down when necessary

Successful people have the ability to slow down when necessary. This is one important habit that they have. When you slow down, it makes you more mindful and more aware of your words, thoughts, actions, decisions, and reactions. And they all define our influence. It makes you become completely aware of your environment.

Create a positive environment

To achieve success, you must create a positive environment where everybody can perform at their best, and create and innovate together. A positive team culture is formed where everyone slows down, employs honesty, listens to learn, and there is effective delegation of tasks. When the work environment is stable and every individual can come to the workplace with their authentic selves, there will be an establishment of the foundation for a positive culture. You can select what type of culture you work in every day, and you can do this by the influence you exert on your team and the actions you take.

Although success has different forms, you must understand your influence if you want to build success that many people can benefit from. As a leader, you are faced with the responsibility of understanding that the influence you have on other individuals matters, and your influence inspires others to do their best work, add to a positive culture, help their clients, and so on. When you help your team members understand how they make contributions to the success of the team and give them a purpose to continue striving, they will do their best to ensure success for the team and themselves.

Types of Influence and How to Use Them

Different types of influence can be used to accomplish goals.

Let us take a look at the different types of influence and how you can use them:

1. **The accessibility influence:** Accessibility influence occurs when a person has access to information or resources that other individuals do not have access to. Access makes the individual able to exert some amount of control over the current situation. If you want to use accessibility influence, you need to identify the information or resources that are accessible to you and not to other individuals.

2. **The authority influence:** The source of authority influence is authority figures, such as teachers, bosses, or

experts. When it comes to influencing others, authority figures usually have a lot of sway and power. You need to first develop your expertise and credibility in the specific area you want to influence before you can be able to use authority influence to accomplish goals. You will be able to get other individuals to easily follow your lead once you have become established as an authority figure. And your followers will help you accomplish your goals.

3. **The social influence:** Social influence is the influence that happens when other people influence someone. This occurs in things like groupthink and peer pressure. It is important that you identify what individuals or groups are most influential over the goal you want to achieve in order to achieve the goals with social influence. After this, you can then make your message appeal to those individuals or groups.

Benefits of Achieving Goals with Influence

Influence is a tool that is often overlooked even though it is powerful when it comes to achieving your goals. Whether you are looking for ways to move ahead in your career, or trying to bring about change in the world, you need to understand that influence can be highly beneficial. You can use influence to accomplish your goals. From spreading knowledge to building relationships with key players, you can use your influence in many ways to achieve tangible outcomes.

We need to first understand what influence really is in order to know how to accomplish goals with it. Influence is an individual's ability to impact the feelings, thoughts, and behaviors of other individuals. However, influence has many different types.

Influence is seen as a process, whereby the influencer, which is a person or thing, affects another person or thing. Others view it as the influencer's property, which allows the influencer to impact others. And others also define it in terms of whether or not the goal that is desired is achieved.

No matter how you may define it, certain elements exist that are important for any act of influence to occur.

These elements include:

A relationship between the influencer and the influencee: For any influence to occur, a relationship must exist between two parties; the influencer and the influencee. This relationship could be a relationship that is personal such as the one that exists between family members or friends, it could be a professional relationship like the relationship between an employee and their boss, or it could be a casual one like the relationship between strangers.

Communication between the influencer and the influencee: Both the influencer and the influencee must have some form of communication, which could be through verbal communication or nonverbal communication.

Influence is quite powerful when it comes to using it to achieve professional and personal goals. When influence is effectively used, it is capable of helping you achieve your objectives. It does this by convincing other individuals to support your decisions, actions, or ideas.

Achieving goals with influence has many benefits which include:

1. **Enhanced reputation and credibility:** When you use influence to accomplish your goals, it is capable of enhancing your reputation and credibility. This is the case because individuals will notice that you are able to convince other individuals to offer you support for your ideas, thereby making you appear more trustworthy and competent.

2. **You have a high rate of achieving success:** You have a high chance of succeeding if you achieve goals with influence, than if you try to achieve the goals without influence. This happens because you can tap into the support and resources of the people who have faith in your vision.

3. **Your relationships improve:** You can improve your relationships with other individuals by using your influence. This is the case because these individuals have respect for your ability to persuade them and this will increase the likelihood of them working with you in the future.

4. **Your impact is greater:** You can make a greater impact by using influence to achieve goals than if you don't use influence. This happens because your results will be amplified as actions get other people's backing.

Risks of Achieving Goals with Influence

There are many risks associated with using influence to accomplish goals. These risks include the potential for wasting resources and time if the goals cannot be achieved, causing harm more than good if the goals fail, losing credibility as a result of the influence not being used appropriately or wisely, and making a negative impact on other individuals if the goals are accomplished at their expense.

Ensure that you carefully consider each of these risks before achieving any goal with influence. If you want to achieve goals with influence, you need to define what you intend to achieve, do some research on the individuals who are influencers in your niche or field, link up with the influencers, develop relationships with them, and then use your influence to accomplish the goals you have.

Influence can help us achieve our goals as it is incredibly powerful. When you have a full understanding of how influence works and how to use effective strategies, you can harness the power to achieve your goals. Whether you are motivating yourself or other individuals, trying to persuade an individual to support a cause, or you are negotiating a deal that is better for you, you can use the principles of influence in various situations. With dedication and practice, any individual can learn how to use influence in the best ways possible and successfully achieve the outcomes they desire.

CHAPTER 4
Influence: The Key To Leadership

When it comes to becoming a successful leader, influence is important. An organization's success relies on many skills, attributes, and experiences of leaders, and having the ability to influence other individuals in an empowering and compassionate way, is a skill that you need to have.

A self-aware leader knows how to develop this skill of influencing other individuals in a way that is helpful to their team. This means that they know how to study the environment and influence it accordingly. They know how to use influence to motivate other people and inspire them to become successful along with them. Influential people don't leave things undone. They are used to getting things done and they motivate other individuals to also get things done.

You need to see influence through the lens of being a servant leader to others, to help them with their development and growth.

You will find these tips helpful:

Look at the big picture

While working with your team, you need to stay focused on the big picture. This is important because how you lead is directly connected to the vision of your company. There is a need for you to always think strategically and be proactive. You need to stay steps ahead of the curve, as it will help you provide direction for your people. The direction you provide will always be results-oriented and focused on moving the company forward.

Remember, as you move higher in the ranks of leadership, you will need to keep your eyes on the big picture, and then connect your people to the vision you have.

Set clear expectations

You need to set expectations that are clear and provide a practical guide. When there is no clarity, there will be confusion and nothing will get done. When you make assumptions, you compromise productivity, and the results your team will provide will not be excellent.

On the other hand, when you maintain healthy two-way communication, your team gets the opportunity to ask you any questions and get clarity about what you expect from them before they even start working on the task at hand. When your team feels emotionally supported, their work will be efficient and high quality with no mediocre results.

Use credibility, competency, and confidence to influence

Credibility, competency, and confidence will help you boost your ability to influence and establish credibility. Connect the dots for your people when you are communicating with them by giving them real examples of what it looks like to meet expectations and even exceed them.

Be collaborative and empowering. When you use this approach in working with your teams, the power of your influence is strengthened and you enable other individuals to share the input they have as well.

Maintain regular communication

You will have a good start by following the advice above, however, you must ensure that you check in regularly with your team to ensure that they complete their tasks.

Some individuals may be more challenged than others, and some may possess different experience levels, but if you ensure that you check on them to make sure that they have everything they need for their work, you are displaying your strong leadership skills. Encouraging them to share progress updates of their work at regular intervals is even better. This will make your team confident enough to take action, ask questions when necessary, and complete tasks efficiently. This is all about setting your team up for success.

Be ready to make adjustments

There will always be differences in opinion in any workplace environment. You need to be ready to handle this whenever issues like this come up as a leader. Allow your head to lead and not your heart. When you keep your emotions in check and stick with the facts, issues will get resolved well and in a timely manner as well.

A good leader encourages their followers to have their own voice. Your job as a leader is to ensure that everyone is aligned with the bigger vision of the organization, no matter the situation, but also encourage effective two-way communication.

How Leaders Influence Their Team

Everything you say and do influences the people around you. If you do your best to ensure that your approach to influence originates from a place of compassion, open-mindedness, and authenticity, you are helping your people and your organization, and you are also helping yourself to accomplish greater success levels.

You need to be able to leverage your influence to help your followers thrive. Good managers become true leaders by developing influence with their teams. When you have strong connections with team members with influence, you will be able to build high-performance teams.

As a leader who motivates their team to increase their productivity, you need to depend on more than the positional authority that you get from a job title. You need to be able to convince the people you lead to follow you, because they want to follow you, and not because they have to follow you.

Authenticity is important when it comes to establishing a strong relationship with employees. Leaders are able to build influence with their followers because it conveys openness, transparency, consistency, and honesty.

It also shows members of the team that their leaders are comfortable with them and can reveal their true selves to them, which gives the employees a positive experience and increases engagement.

But how are people influenced by leaders, and how do the leaders ensure that influence is mutually beneficial, positive, inclusive, authentic, and not reliant on positional authority?

Other individuals are influenced by leaders in positive ways by building relationships that are trust-based with them, promoting a culture of accountability, valuing people over profits, committing to the people's growth, maintaining authority while also offering the people autonomy, and articulating a vision that connects the people with a shared sense of purpose.

Leaders influence other individuals in ways that support a work environment that is productive and respectful, promote teamwork at every level, and create the conditions that are necessary to achieve success without causing harm to the well-being of team members.

Leaders influence by doing the following:

Building strong trust-based relationships

One great way that leaders influence other individuals is by building strong trust-based relationships with members of the team.

Trust is one thing that is important for any team. It helps employees develop strong relationships with their colleagues and helps leaders build rapport with their employees.

How well an employee performs, the level of productivity they bring, and the organization's profitability are dependent on the level of trust the employee has in their leader. When trust is absent, it can result in toxic work environments and will make employees leave the company.

Good communication, collaboration, and good teamwork can result from a high level of trust. Employees are also encouraged to engage more with their work and have better performance.

Leaders develop authentic connections with members of their team and build trust by leading with honesty, compassion, self-awareness, and transparency. They also form connections by honing their emotional intelligence.

The meaningful and authentic connections and trust-based relationships that leaders have with members of the team create success for the organization without being detrimental to the leaders or the people's well-being.

It is important to build meaningful relationships with the members of your team and other individuals inside and outside the organization. An inclusive environment with an open-door policy is what leaders need to create so that it can make the members of the team feel comfortable when it comes to sharing their experiences. You must be willing to get to know people and also allow them to know you on a personal level.

Maintaining a work environment that is inclusive and positive, where every member of the team feels valued, heard, and committed to the vision of the organization assists leaders in building positive influence and trust with employees in ways that encourage them to continue performing well.

Holding yourself and your employees accountable

Encouraging the members of your team and allowing them to work with autonomy makes them take accountability. As it is with autonomy, leaders have to provide the members of their team with the tools to keep themselves accountable. Unfortunately, this is not always done.

Some workers are not clear on the expectations of their organization. They are not able to take responsibility or align their work with expected results, the behavior of their leader is one factor that impacts responsibility in their organization.

Feedback helps employees know what their organization or leader expects of them and how they can achieve the goals they are expected to achieve. So, you need to give your employees feedback as it is important for increasing productivity. However, some leaders give feedback without expectations, which is something critical.

If you don't give your employees the clarity to assume ownership and perform great work, you can't expect them to take accountability for whatever the results are. As a leader, you are responsible for your team and you have to guide them toward achieving the goals that have been set. When the goals that were set are not met, they have to be willing to acknowledge the role they played in the process and also learn from the mistakes they have made.

This creates an opportunity for leaders to show that they assume ownership as leaders. When this clarity is provided by leaders through frequent feedback, they are showing their own accountability for setting expectations and motivating their employees to hold themselves accountable when it comes to meeting expectations.

Keep your focus on making sure that job expectations are clear and the organization's goals and the role of employees in accomplishing the goals are clearly communicated rather than punishing the employees for not achieving the results that are expected. When your team doesn't meet expectations, don't just react, but ensure that your employees are getting recognition when they achieve the required results.

Committing to growth

Studies show that an absence of opportunities for advancement makes people quit their jobs.

Employees need to work on increasing their knowledge and building new skills to perform better at their jobs and grow. People will not be happy in jobs that have no clear path to growth.

As a leader, you need to be committed to the growth of the members of your team if you expect them to accompany you on the journey. You can't expect the members of your team to grow in their roles, and move into roles that have higher levels if you fail to give them opportunities to grow and the encouragement to use these opportunities.

Providing learning opportunities, whether the training is in-person or online, reimbursement of tuition, or leadership development, can meet the growth needs of employees and help them grow professionally.

Leaders also assist employees in growing personally by providing them with volunteering opportunities that incorporate community involvement into their lives in the workplace. This creates a positive working environment and boosts employee morale.

Volunteer opportunities that boost morale and volunteerism are important for the well-being of employees.

Putting other individuals first

When leaders practice selfless leadership and consider the needs of the members of their team first, the leaders are more effective. A person who serves their employees well will also be good at serving their customers.

Leaders who serve their employees are referred to as servant leaders. The servant leader not only leads but also serves the people they lead by building positive influence with the members of the team and making investments in their success.

This is what servant leadership is about. The servant-leader is first a servant. They have the natural feeling of wanting to serve first and not because they desire wealth, fame, influence, or power.

There is a need for good leaders to become good servants first. Some characteristics are associated with servant leadership, which help leaders when it comes to serving and leading well, and they include conceptualization, awareness, foresight, listening, stewardship, empathy, persuasion, healing, building community, and commitment to the people's growth.

These characteristics help with forming authentic relationships with the members of the team and maintaining a work environment that is harmonious and has a winning culture where the workers grow and accomplish goals without job dissatisfaction, poor well-being, and burnout.

Being in a position of authority and also offering autonomy

A leader's effectiveness is reliant on their ability to build influence which is beyond positional authority.

Influence is the key to successful leadership. It is not authority. For leaders to relate well with others, they must be close enough, and for leaders to motivate others, they must be far enough. If you desire to be respected by people as a leader, you need to show them that they can thrive and survive even without you. Effective leaders do this by providing their employees autonomy.

Workers are increasingly desiring more flexibility in the form of autonomy, and this is tied to motivation as well. Studies have shown that employees who are motivated are more oriented towards independence and autonomy and are more self-driven than less motivated employees.

Autonomy varies from one business to another, but the aim of providing employees autonomy is that it meets the needs of an employee to work in ways that are more self-directed and provides them with the opportunity to assume ownership of their responsibilities and roles. And it does this no matter the organization.

Great leaders provide the members of their team with the necessary tools for their work and also give their team autonomy to achieve their full potential. These leaders don't micromanage.

When you provide workers with the autonomy they want, you are forming relationships that are strong and trust-based with your employees and also encouraging them to be accountable and take ownership. It is this sense of ownership that motivates the employees to perform great work.

Working with a vision statement

A vision statement provides direction. It is an important part of planning in an organization and is not just a sentence that is found on an organization's website.

The vision of an organization provides a purpose for the organization's employees. It is supported by its mission and gives the employees a goal to work towards.

Vision helps individuals visualize their goals and work towards achieving those goals. A mental image is created by the vision statement. The statement looks forward and the image it creates is of the state that the organization desires to achieve. It is aspirational and inspirational and employees should be challenged by it.

You can create a vision statement by first answering these questions:

What is the problem that the organization wants to solve?

What direction is the organization going?

What would the organization look like a decade from now if it achieves all the strategic goals it has?

Employees need to be committed to helping the organization achieve the mission that the founders of the organization have set and then do their work well. This is what makes it important for the vision to be articulated by leadership.

Leaders don't only have to know the "why;" they also need to be able to let their team know the "why."

Everyone may not understand the why behind your organization or team even though it may be obvious to you. So, don't assume that they know it. Not everyone knows where you want to be or what you want to achieve one year or two years from now. So, the leader must give them that information. And you can do this by coming up with a narrative, to create a story that is compelling so that people may see how they can connect within that.

Leaders explain the organization's vision and then reinforce it with the members of the team by making them find their work meaningful by connecting it to the higher purpose of the organization and recognizing their work's impact.

Team members are united by a shared sense of purpose, and this creates a positive work environment that favors collaboration, maximizes the team's efforts and all employees work in harmony to achieve the organization's vision.

Morale, trust, performance, and overall job satisfaction are improved when employees feel a strong commitment to the vision of the organization and also feel a shared sense of purpose with their colleagues.

Leaders define and also reinforce the sense of purpose of their employees by tying it to the work that the employees perform each day and the organization's mission and vision. You can help the members of your team find purpose in the work they are doing for the organization by setting expectations that are connected to the broader vision of the organization and expectations that reflect the organization's core values and culture.

When you are able to use purposeful work to embed culture in your organization, there is also a clarification and reinforcement of the vision with employees in ways that improve values alignment.

More About Leadership Influence

Professional leadership has to do with guiding an entire department or a small team of employees in completing different tasks and projects. Influencing your team or department can affect the way workers feel about their tasks and how they feel in their roles, and you can create a positive experience with this opportunity. When you understand how effective leadership influence is, you will be able to apply it to your workplace. You will find leadership influence quite beneficial in your organization.

Leadership influence is an individual's ability to change attitudes, beliefs, or values about a topic. As you become more experienced as a leader, you can learn this skill. A leader is able to use their speaking ability and knowledge to offer new information or a new perspective to a team or an audience. Leaders who are successful when it comes to influencing their audience may change the minds of their audiences about a topic because of the way the leaders present their information.

An individual with leadership influence can understand what creates a sense of urgency and moves people to create change. If an audience can trust their leaders, they will be more open to being influenced.

A leader can create trust with their audience in the following ways:

Communicating your interests: When you communicate your work interests with a positive experience and with passion, you can show the people you are trying to influence that you are passionate about what you are talking about.

Forming connections with your team members: Connect with the members of your team or your audience to understand what motivates them, what they need, and their values.

Building credibility: Credibility can be established if your motives are clear and you are honest. You can also establish credibility if you demonstrate the knowledge you have with research and share your findings with other individuals.

Staying open to different perspectives: It's helpful for the members of your team or your audience to be aware that their leader is open to listening to different perspectives. You can make this happen by asking them to share their thoughts concerning what you said or by giving them the chance to ask questions.

Remaining accountable: You can remain accountable to develop trust with other individuals because it allows them to see your commitment to your work. You can make sure that you set clear expectations as well as checkpoints for updates with the members of your team and your audience.

What makes leadership influence important is that you can influence a person or many people, like the members of your team at work or an auditorium of people listening as you speak to them. Leaders who are used to influencing other individuals may inspire new changes, strategies, or ideas within an organization. Organizations are able to reach their goals with this type of leadership and it also helps employees to experience more satisfaction with their job. Employees can be motivated by influence to work hard and accomplish the goals of the company.

As a leader, you can use the following characteristics of effective leadership influence in your management:

1. Being open

Being open and encouraging is important as a leader because it makes other individuals share the ideas they have with you. You can offer help to each other as you do your work together. When you are leading a team meeting, you will find it beneficial to ask other individuals to share their ideas if no individual is speaking. This can make them see that you value their input and that they are allowed to share their thoughts during the meeting. You will also find it beneficial because you can help improve the company by using the skills of the team.

2. Providing value

The member of a team or an audience can apply value to their lives, and this can be done whether it is tangible or intangible. You will find it helpful to incorporate the values you have into your actions and words when you are influencing other individuals as a leader. If you have a team that you are managing, you can help finish a project or complete a task before its deadline, which may make you valuable in being a team player and helping others. If your team members are looking for advice for advancement in their careers, you can work with them individually. When you add value, the people listening will be empowered to share with others what they have learned.

3. Positive attitude

A person's attitude is the way they feel and think about something or an individual and how it reflects through their behavior. Having a positive attitude can be beneficial when you are influencing other individuals. A person's attitude can affect how other individuals around them also feel about something or someone. For instance, if you have a positive attitude toward implementing a new strategy in your workplace, the members of your team may also welcome the idea and feel optimistic.

4. Sharing knowledge

A leader will find it helpful to commit to continuing their education and sharing their knowledge. This can be done by taking additional training courses that the organization provides for its employees. When you share your expertise, the members of your team may be inspired to change their strategies or to continue their education to complete a task. You and the members of your team can find it beneficial to commit to continuing your education in your field. This shows that there is still a lot you can do to gain an increase in knowledge within your industry and increase your job performance.

5. Effective listening

Listening can help you build a stronger connection with other individuals. As a leader, when you listen to an audience or the members of your team, there may be a high likelihood of creating influence. Listening to other individuals can allow you to hear about the desires and values that people have, thereby helping you to develop your leadership skills in those particular areas. When you are trying to influence people, you will find this helpful because you can discuss interests or ideas that they find relevant.

6. Efficient time management

While it is important to plan in the workplace, practicing mindfulness is also important. Mindfulness involves completely paying attention to the present moment that you are experiencing without worrying about the future or the past. A leader who has the desire to influence the members of their team can encourage the team members to stay focused on the things that they know that they can complete today. Productivity can be increased by getting your team to focus on those things that they can complete during a workday. Their engagement in their tasks can increase and they can complete the tasks quickly and efficiently.

7. Being passionate

Passion motivates individuals to work toward their professional and personal goals. When you are excited about an idea, it can motivate other individuals. This can make them change their perspective or act on your idea. This part of leadership influence is important because it motivates individuals to continue learning new things and developing in their careers and as a person.

Leadership Influence Benefits and Examples

Let us take a look at some of the benefits that leadership influence has:

It encourages education: Sharing your knowledge and expertise with other individuals can give them the inspiration to educate themselves more about a particular topic or do further research to understand the topic better.

It promotes change: An opportunity exists for you to encourage others to request change at work or to create change if they are passionate about what you are talking about. This is good for organizations if the change makes the process easier for others to complete or helps them reach their goals.

It helps with motivation: You can ask the employees what they require to be successful in their role. This way, you can influence others and increase their motivation to do their work. This can provide them with the support and tools to perform their job well.

The following are some examples of leadership influence in the workplace:

First example: Effective listening influence

As a leader, there may be times when a member of your team is not performing well in the role they are meant to play in the team. The member of the team may not be performing their tasks well or they may be missing deadlines, thereby slowing the project timeline down. Creating time to discuss with them and address their behavior will be helpful.

This can be done by asking the individual how you can support them. Letting them know that you appreciate them is also important. Let them know that the rest of the team values them and the team depends on them for the completion of tasks on time. This will motivate them.

Second example: Positive attitude influence

As the holidays draw near, the members of your team may consider it challenging to give themselves the motivation to complete their work. You can help to motivate your team to complete their projects by using your influence as a leader. This can be done by asking them about the areas of their struggle and how you can help them. When you assist your team on a project, explain a new strategy that they can try, or reassign tasks, you are helping them.

Third example: Efficient time management influence

The members of your team are working on a marketing project and the deadline is moved up a week earlier by the client, thereby causing an increase in the work hours as the team members work on weekends and even into the evening. As an influential leader, you can work with the team during the extra hours to help them meet the deadline. This will show the team that you are a part of the team. When you help them perform some of their tasks, it shows your commitment. Your team will feel motivated to finish their tasks when you share the benefits of early completion of projects.

CHAPTER 5
Building Relationships

A good relationship is capable of protecting you from failure in your business and life. You must have heard people say that behind every great man, is a great woman. You can reverse the phrase nowadays and the point would remain the same. Good relationships can make you successful in the workplace and life.

This is important for individuals who are single to contemplate and for individuals who are in a relationship. Single individuals might consider the fact that having a life partner is beneficial. Individuals who are in a relationship need to have an understanding that whatever they do can make or break the success of their counterpart's success in their place of work.

You need to know the following:

We can receive the motivation to do well.

We desire to make the people we love proud. If that doesn't motivate you, another thing that can motivate you may be that you provide for the family and don't want to do anything that will let them down.

A partner can remind you about the things you love about your job.

When you get back from work and say that you are going to quit work, your loved one can talk to you calmly about the situation and help you calm down.

Your partner can refresh your memory about the most important thing.

Every one of us has goals in life, but living in the moment may be what is most important and not just achieving the goals. When family members or friends are in town but you want to stay late in the office because you think it is the right thing to do, your loved one can encourage you to create time for the individuals in your life.

A romantic relationship has the ability to develop our confidence.

Maintaining a healthy relationship, as well as winning a person over, can make us have a good feeling about ourselves. We will appear confident wherever we go.

Things go smoothly

When things are going smoothly at home, other aspects of your life seem to work well too. Your performance at work will improve if you are not weighed down by relationship problems.

A partner can be a lifesaver and pick up the slack.

Sometimes you might be very busy in your workplace. You may have a partner who can pick up the slack at home during your busy time, whether it be doing the laundry or making dinner for everyone at home.

Being in a romantic relationship can make you look your best.

This might be something like taking time to do your hair or going to the gym more often. Whatever you decide to give your attention to in order to look good for your partner, you will discover that it will also pay off in your workplace. The individuals who appear more pulled together have a high likelihood of being offered more promotions and opportunities, and there is also the fact that people usually feel good when they look their best.

Your partner celebrates with you:

Your loved one should be the biggest cheerleader you have. Your partner may not be in agreement with all that you do, but they should agree with your work. Your successes need to be celebrated and having someone to celebrate with you is helpful.

Your loved one can help you with your ideas

If you have a lot of ideas in your head at any particular moment, you will find it helpful to discuss them with someone either to get trusted feedback or for the sake of hearing them out loud. Some of the ideas you are having may be silly and having someone that can tell you that the ideas are silly is good.

A partner has the ability to provide an outside perspective.

Most times, we find ourselves caught up in a situation, making it difficult for us to have perspective. A person who is outside of the situation and who is also close to you might help you look at the situation from a different angle and even find a good solution.

A partner can help to relieve your stress

Have you ever had the opportunity to laugh at a funny movie with an individual or had a shoulder rub after working the whole day at work? These are just some ways that work-related stress can be relieved by a partner. This can help you unwind as well as recharge for the following workday.

Success Relies on Relationships

Time may not be enough for you to do things. But in an era of telecommuting, social networking, and virtual meetings, when work is concerned, relationships usually get sacrificed.

This is a mistake

If you desire to achieve great things in your career, in business, or management, just focusing on working non-stop without building relationships is the worst thing you can do. Success needs relationships. This includes the relationships you have with your peers, customers, employees, boss, management, and everyone in your workplace.

This does not mean only working relationships; it involves the personal relationships you have with these people, where they actually connect with you personally and not only professionally.

Building relationships with people is not about wasting their time. In fact, wasting people's time is not a good idea because people have a lot to do with their time these days. But if you connect with others and you are open, genuine, and sensitive to the boundaries of people, everything will be alright.

Your success relies more on those interpersonal work relationships that are more important than you even realize.

Any entrepreneur or CEO will tell you that the network that they have built is their biggest asset. They get opportunities from their network. And when networking is involved, social networking is different from doing it old school. Having a personal relationship with an individual builds trust and sets you apart from others.

Information is power, and strong relationships make getting information easier. The information could be about an upcoming promotion opportunity, budget cuts, a big customer, or a major project. When important stuff is involved, it will be difficult to get something valuable from a person who doesn't trust you. You have to give something to get something.

Relationships usually help people get through tough times. A personal relationship is capable of helping you win business deals, keep your job, or get whatever you need. It can make a difference when you find yourself in challenging situations. It also means you have an individual that you can lean on. It's not a good idea to try leaning on an individual that you don't know much about.

Types of Relationships

All kinds of relationships are important. You may not have known this in your childhood days, but as you grow older, you see that they are important and powerful. We experience different types of relationships in our lives. Some of the relationships may be romantic and most of them won't be romantic.

If you are a performer or athlete, you will understand that relationships play a major part in your success.

When you put in the effort to build healthy relationships, it can impact your success the way a physical skill can.

Performers and athletes find themselves faced with four types of relationships which are important. There are also many other relationships, such as relationships with friends, trainers, and teachers.

But, the four types of relationships we will talk about are going to impact your business greatly. You will gain valuable knowledge when you learn to understand these relationship types and the best ways to develop them.

Before we discuss these relationships, take some time to think for yourself. What relationships do you have in your life right now, both personal and professional, that would lead to more success and happiness in your life if given the necessary attention?

If you have never given this a thought, I'm afraid you would have missed out on many relationships and lost opportunities as a result. It can be challenging to build relationships, and it is even more difficult for introverts.

If you don't feel confident and you feel shy when it comes to talking to people, especially people you are just getting to meet for the first time, you will put more pressure on yourself by worrying about building a relationship. It can be difficult, but when you are able to cultivate such relationships, you will discover that the benefits far outweigh the discomfort.

These four types of relationships include relationships with your teammates, coaches, parents, and yourself.

When you nourish each of these four relationships, it will impact your career and help you achieve success. Let us start by discussing the relationship with your parents.

Relationship with parents

The relationship you have with your parents is the first relationship that greatly impacts your success. For many of us, this relationship is the first one we experience. The quality of this relationship will play a major role in our moving ahead in life.

How is the relationship you have with your parents? How would you rate it? Do you feel as though you are close to them and can get support from them?

The relationship you share with your parents can sometimes be tricky. This is the case because we do not get the opportunity to choose our parents. You are stuck with the parents you have.

This means you have less control over the relationship as a child. You are mostly under the care of your parents as a young child. However, as you grow older, it is within your power to keep the relationship intact.

The relationship you have with your parents can help shape your professional life. If you are an athlete, this relationship plays a major role in your life as an athlete.

You must remember the impact that your parents have on your career as you move ahead in your career. What characteristics and attributes did your parents instill in you?

Not every relationship with parents will be positive. Sometimes, we can develop a few traits that are not so helpful and this may be done unintentionally.

Some positive traits that you may experience from the relationship you share with your parents include perseverance, a growth mindset, a strong work ethic, a healthy view of failure, high self-confidence, high self-worth, self-discipline, and self-motivation. As your relationship with your parents continues to grow, they provide more support and teach you more lessons. The more support your parents give you and the more lessons you learn from them, the higher your likelihood of developing these positive traits. You may adopt these positive and healthy characteristics from your parents.

Low self-worth, low self-confidence, fixed mindset, perfectionism, tendencies to blame others, unhealthy view of failure, fear of making a mistake, and anxiety are some negative traits that you may experience from the relationship that you have shared with your parents.

It's usually tricky to start talking about the different ways a child can be negatively influenced by a parent. That's why we need to know it could be unintentional.

A parent does not intentionally prepare their child to blame other individuals for their mistakes nor do they intentionally prepare them to have low confidence. As we grow up, we pick up the mindsets and views of the people who are close to us. So, if you have parents with any of these tendencies, they will likely become a part of your way of thinking.

Now let us talk about when the relationship's quality with your parents rests more on your shoulders.

As you grow older, you can ensure a healthy relationship through communication. If you want the understanding and support of your parents, there must be a level of transparency. Being open to your parents about your goals, desires, and any challenges that may come up is what this means.

You have to be open to support to keep your parents as a shoulder you can lean on.

Relationship with coach

The next relationship that impacts your success is the relationship with your coach. Although it is good to build a healthy relationship with your coaches, it is not an easy thing to do. If you are a reserved and shy person, you may not understand that it is important to build relationships with your coaches. You might even say the coaches don't need to be your friend since they are your coaches.

Although this may be true, being your coach's friend should not be your aim, but building a relationship with them.

A positive relationship with your coach can give you the following benefits:

Playing becomes enjoyable: Playing becomes much more enjoyable and you have a positive playing experience when you get along with your coach and the relationship is strong. This also results in a better experience overall in your sport.

Increased confidence in skills: When you have a positive relationship with your coach, it will result in increased confidence in your skills. You will be able to communicate the weaknesses you have and your coach will help you work on those weaknesses.

Embracing mistakes: When you know that you have a strong relationship with your coach, you embrace your mistakes instead of allowing them to weigh you down. If your coach is supportive, you understand that it is necessary to make mistakes to become better as a player.

More opportunities: Connections are important, even though it may be hard for you to believe it. When you have a good relationship with your coach, there will be a higher chance that they will play you more and this will help with advancement in your levels.

You will have a mindset of improving: If the relationship you have with your coach is an unhealthy one, it will leave you with the need to perform. Every game and practice will become a performance. If the relationship you have with your coach is a healthy one, you will know that your coach's job is to help you get better as a player. Now, you will stay focused on getting better instead of proving yourself.

You and your coach should invest time in the relationship. They have to want the best for you. If you have a coach who is chronically negative and distant or has a negative influence, it will be difficult to build a relationship with them.

If your coach is someone who has an overall bad influence, you can switch teams or try different options. Your level of play will be improved if the relationship you share with your coach is strong. You will also have a more enjoyable experience. Ensure that you find yourself a coach with whom you can build such a relationship.

Relationship between athlete and teammate

For the relationship between athlete and teammate, the focus changes from authority figures to our peers. It is important to develop a healthy relationship with your teammates as you will enjoy its many benefits.

Cohesiveness is built within the team. You must have known teams or found yourself on teams that just seemed to click. These teams often appear to be successful. The relationships and bonds that they build result in more chemistry and they get higher levels of play.

Enjoyment is another reason why relationships with teammates are important. If you have some teammates that you don't get along with or teammates that you don't like, that is capable of making the time you spend on the team dreadful.

You may have had teammates you could not stand which resulted in less joy. Of course, not every individual is going to be close friends with everyone. But you can still build a healthy relationship with those particular teammates that you don't really like.

Another reason, which is important to athletes, involves competition. What goal do you have when you go to practice? Your everyday goal should be to make improvements.

How can you increase your rate of improvement? You can do this by having a competition that is healthy with your teammates and encouraging each other to work harder.

Don't avoid competition of this type. Do not stay away from another teammate whom you fear seems better than you. Ensure that you develop your relationship with them.

The healthy competition going on between you and your teammate will force you to improve. Also, as you get closer to them, you will also learn more from each other and help each other.

Look at your teammates and check for relationships that are strong enough for you to build upon, and also notice the relationships that you need to work to improve.

If this is done, there will be a skyrocket in the level of your play as well as the fulfillment you get in your sport.

Relationship with yourself

Wait, is it possible to have a relationship with yourself?

Although this may sound strange, the relationship that will impact your performance the most and also impact the other three relationships we have talked about is the relationship you have with yourself.

If you are not sure of the meaning of this, think about how much you talk to yourself daily. Try to speak to yourself more than you speak to others in a day.

While you may not be speaking out loud to yourself, you might speak to yourself through your thoughts. How you see yourself is also important; it is not only how you talk to yourself that matters.

Have you ever had thoughts about your perception of yourself? This is referred to as self-image. When sport is involved, do you see yourself as a great player or an average player?

How do you see your ability to get back up from failure? Do you believe you lack what it takes to move forward? Or do you see yourself as a person who stands strong in the midst of adversity?

You need to focus on how you speak to yourself and how you view yourself to maintain a quality relationship with yourself. Whether you get to have a healthy relationship with yourself or an unhealthy one will be largely dependent on the level of self-worth you have, your emotional intelligence, your motivation, whether your self-confidence is high or low, your work ethic and self-discipline, and your ability to handle failure and adversity.

All these characteristics are valuable when it comes to your performance as well as your life.

When you have a healthy relationship with yourself, you will reap the benefits of the relationship. So, how can you build a healthy relationship with yourself? Let us discuss that.

Cultivating a Positive Relationship with Yourself

When you want to cultivate a healthier relationship with yourself, the first thing you need to do is to recognize your ability to do so. If you believe that it is stupid to cultivate a relationship with yourself, that mindset will not take you far in life.

So, you first need to acknowledge that you have a relationship with yourself, and you should do your best to make that relationship a positive one. You need to pay attention to the image you hold of yourself and how you talk to yourself.

You need to do the following:

Focus on the way you talk to yourself

You need to start focusing on the way you talk to yourself. Countless thoughts flood your mind daily, and this is what makes it impossible to be consciously aware of every thought at every moment.

Instead, you can start by using some minutes to pick out the negative phrases you often use. Every one of us has phrases or statements that are repetitive.

The negative words you use may be boring and plain, but they can do wonders when it comes to destroying the relationship you have with yourself. Could you imagine yourself using some negative words when speaking to your teammates? It can get them offended. If you are aware that your teammates do not appreciate anybody speaking to them in that manner, why talk to yourself in that manner?

Identify the negative statements and phrases that you are always saying to yourself. Once you are aware of those negative statements and phrases, you need to come up with some positive alternatives and start making changes to the way you speak to yourself.

Change your perception of yourself

As soon as you start working on self-talk, it will alter your self-image. Your self-image will improve as you start speaking better to yourself.

You can use visualization to alter your self-perception. Look for one area of your life that you desire to change the image you hold about yourself currently. An example can be your ability to handle failure.

If you currently hold the belief that you are really terrible at managing adversity, you can change your perception and see yourself positively responding to your failure.

Mental imagery and visualization come into play here. Take out five or ten minutes every day to spend with yourself. Close your eyes and visualize what you want to see about yourself. See yourself giving a positive response to failure in the way that you would like to respond.

As time passes, your self-image will be improved and this can help you have a healthier relationship with yourself.

Relationships are important. There are different types of relationships, but paying attention to these four is really important. You can see that these relationships include the relationship you have with yourself, your parents, your teammates, and your coaches.

When you focus on these relationships, you will have more self-confidence, higher performance levels, and a more enjoyable and fulfilling experience.

Take a look at the relationships, and try to figure out which of them you need to work on. You might have a weak point in one or more of them. A professional can help you if you are performing below your potential and need help to improve.

CHAPTER 6
The Power Of Skills

Having skills is important for a successful career. What do you understand by skills? Skills can be described as having the knowledge, competency, and ability to complete a given task. Skills are learned or developed through active learning or experience. They make work easier for people. Skills can be something as simple as writing, dancing, or cooking tasty food. Depending upon the nature of work and the need, individuals need to possess different skills. For example, a person working in an organization's finance department should have a good knowledge of accountancy and mathematical calculations. Whereas, a person working in an advertisement agency does not need a good understanding of accountancy. Skills make tasks easy for people in their various fields.

Skills Students Need

1. **Good problem-solving skills:** In addition to all the important skills, students need to have good problem-solving skills as they need to be able to think logically and critically in difficult situations. For example, if the teacher gives the students a group project to work on and one of the members of the team cannot take part in the activity, the other team members should not complain about it but find a solution to the problem.

2. **Computer skills:** As a result of digitalization in the 21st century, there is an increasing need for teachers, students, and everyone to be tech-savvy. From submitting assignments to conducting online classes, computer skills

are important. People even study online and graduate with degrees today. It is important for students to be computer literate or possess good computer skills in order to get themselves prepared to face any future challenges.

3. **Making quick decisions:** Students need to be able to make decisions quickly. This is an important skill that they need to have. Students must make quick decisions as they need to make decisions often. From making choices about the right internships to making choices about the right educational courses, making good decisions is important for students to have a good career.

Importance of Good Skills

1. **Contributes to personal growth:** If a person makes an effort to learn new skills, whether it is for professional or personal reasons, those skills can contribute to their growth. For example, if an individual learns computer skills, they will find it useful even in the future.

2. **Good skills keep you ahead of the game:** Acquiring skills is important as it helps in growth and development. All you need is good skills to find your space in this world that is full of competition. Skills increase your chances of achieving success. For example, if a person wants to apply for a job, they need to do better than many other competitors who possess the same abilities. However, when an individual has some extraordinary skills that are useful, they will stand out amongst their peers.

3. **Helps in a better salary negotiation:** No organization wants to pay people for free. However, if the individuals are capable of bringing profit to the organization with their skills, they would be hired by the organization and

their desired salary offered to them. An individual with good skills has the ability to outshine other competitors and also ace the role the organization has chosen them for.

Apart from these benefits that we have mentioned above, being skillful helps the individual stay satisfied and confident. Everyone who is trying to grow as the world continues to grow needs skill development.

Skills for Career Success

Whether you are a mid-career professional trying to get your next promotion or you just graduated from school and you are trying to figure out how to move ahead in your career, you might be thinking about the skills you need to acquire that will help you get to where you want to go. While developing skills that are specific to your industry is important for your success, soft skills involve how you interact with other individuals in the workplace and how you function there. And while these skills are not easily taught by teachers in a classroom or are not easily measured, every one of us needs these skills. Also, in our fast-changing and more globalized work environment, it is important to have soft skills as they are important for future work

You will need these soft skills if you are looking to accelerate your career:

1. The learnability skill

This is a very important 21st-century skill that is needed to achieve success. Today, new skills emerge fast as the old ones fade, so it is important for one to be willing to learn things, unlearn, and also relearn things. Success is not only about what you know but about developing your skills, expanding your knowledge base and then using the skills and information to tackle whatever is happening.

2. Ability to collaborate

Our world is becoming increasingly hyper-connected, and we now collaborate with others more often. Our projects are getting more complex, so working effectively in a team is becoming increasingly important. As work becomes more global, your ability to share knowledge, collaborate, and contribute to teams that can use a diversity of perspectives and think in ways that everybody can benefit from and contribute to productivity is critical.

3. The skill of resilience

Failures and setbacks are inevitable in life, but what is critical to your success is how you choose to handle them. Resilience is one's ability to bounce back from failures and obstacles. When an individual is resilient, they don't focus on the problems in their life. Instead, they keep their focus on their long-term goals, and they don't lose confidence in their ability to be successful. By helping you face difficulties and challenges, resilience also makes it possible for you to stay positive while handling stress.

4. The skill of creativity

We all need the skill of creativity because employers value employees who can be creative and imagine future possibilities for their organization. Creative employees imagine these possibilities and work to bring their imagination to life. These individuals are curious and ask questions, and this makes them come up with new ideas and solutions.

5. Verbal communication skills

Moving forward in your career is not only based on your actions. You will also have to use strong verbal communication skills at some point in your career to sell other individuals your services, products, or ideas. Whether you want to make a presentation as part of a team project, whether you are trying to explain how valuable you are when you are being considered to be promoted, or you are speaking to an audience, there is a need for you to be able to communicate properly and convey persuasive and strong ideas.

6. The agility skill

As work continues to evolve, agility gets more important. One critical skill that we need is learning to be agile, as tomorrow's problems are not solved by yesterday's solutions. You need to be able to shift and respond accordingly to the industry trends, clients, and the needs of your workplace.

7. Leadership skills

It is important to build the right culture in companies. Having the necessary skills to be able to empower and coach other individuals, and to motivate the people around you to perform their best work is important for success.

8. The skill of empathy

The ability to see things from the perspective of other people and understand their reactions and emotions or the ability to empathize with others, is an important aspect of our interactions with one another. Communicating authentically and genuinely with other individuals is important, and empathy can even help you demonstrate to other individuals that they are heard and seen even in situations when you disagree with them on elements of a project.

9. Written communication skills

We live in a time of social media, but it is still necessary to have good written communication skills when it comes to your career. Whether you are communicating with a client, sending professional emails, or trying to deliver a business plan, you must be able to communicate accurately, quickly, and effectively.

10. The skill of negotiation

Whether you are finalizing a deal with a client, having salary discussions, or trying to find common ground with your colleagues during an office project, having effective and strong negotiation skills is highly important. Once you are good at negotiating, it helps you to reach goals and also build relationships, which is important when it comes to having a successful career.

11. Problem-solving skills

Do you usually go beyond the work you have been assigned and instead, use more data, facts, and knowledge to see any available gaps and solve problems? It is important that you have good problem-solving skills as employers value individuals who can handle challenges on their own or tackle challenges as effective team members by stating the issues, brainstorming a variety of alternatives, sharing your thoughts, and then making the right decisions.

12.   Technology skills

Technology is rapidly changing, so it is important to keep up with technology even beyond the technical skills that are required for your job. This is necessary because of the tools that help you brand yourself, differentiate yourself in the market, manage your career, and build the vital relationships that you need to achieve success.

Regardless of the career path that you have chosen, building your soft skills is important as it helps to differentiate you from other individuals when there is competition.

CHAPTER 7
The Relationship Between Gratitude And Success

Gratitude is powerful. When you appreciate success, it can bring you more success. Gratitude attracts joy, positivity, and abundance into our lives.

Imagine a life where you celebrate every milestone, every small victory you achieve, and each setback you experience acts as a catalyst for your growth. This is what gratitude is, and this mindset has the ability to multiply our achievements and transform our lives.

When we stay focused on appreciating the successes we have achieved, we open ourselves up to welcome more positivity into our lives.

Gratitude is a great weapon for success. Embracing this weapon of success can improve your well-being and help you experience continued success in your personal life and career. Gratitude can help any individual become successful.

You need to know the following:

1. Gratitude makes relationships stronger

You might not be where you are in your life today without the support and guidance of your mentors, colleagues, and teachers. So, you need to express your gratitude to every individual who helped you get to where you are today.

You can show them appreciation by giving them gifts to thank them.

They will appreciate the small gesture. People often appreciate when the efforts they have put in are recognized. You will notice their enthusiasm and willingness to help you again if you need their help in the future.

Gratitude is powerful when it comes to strengthening relationships. When you show appreciation to the people who have helped you in one way or the other, it creates meaningful connections, opens the doors to opportunities, and encourages future collaboration. Individuals have a high likelihood of offering encouragement and help when they feel appreciated, and this can lead to a network that is supportive and aids your success.

You need other individuals to help you attain your goals, and the best way you can easily build strong relationships is by showing gratitude for the help they have rendered to you.

2. Gratitude makes us focus on the positive

You may have a lot of stressful moments as you perform extracurricular activities, attend classes, and prepare for other school activities. When you always practice gratitude, it helps you stay positive. You acknowledge and celebrate every step you are taking forward instead of thinking about the things you are yet to achieve. You stop being overwhelmed with negative feelings and you start feeling motivated that you can do it right and start seeing the challenges as growth opportunities. Gratitude trains your mind to stay focused on the good things you have in your life instead of focusing on what is wrong or what you don't have. Your motivation and confidence are boosted by this positive outlook, empowering you to pick up new challenges and strive to achieve greater things.

3. Gratitude makes decision-making better

Throughout your life, you will find yourself having to make important decisions every day. And this can be intimidating. When you have gratitude in mind, you become more confident in your decision-making ability and become more comfortable.

If a plan that you made was rejected or if you made a mistake, gratitude comes and reminds you that this is an opportunity to learn from your mistake and do it better the next time.

Gratitude is empowering and helps you make better decisions. It helps you reframe your mistakes as opportunities to learn new things, and gratitude helps you to move past your failures fast and make more confident decisions. You stop being clouded by fear of failure or doubt and start believing that any outcome of the decisions you make will be valuable.

You are also more likely to come up with creative solutions and explore new possibilities when your mindset is a positive one. As a result, the decisions you make create new paths for your success in the future.

4. Gratitude promotes resilience

Life may be stressful, but gratitude can help you strike a healthy balance between doing your work and also appreciating where you are in your journey. Showing gratitude for the things you have accomplished, such as passing an exam that was difficult for you to write or getting positive feedback for an important thing, can help you come back quickly from any setbacks you have experienced and keep a positive attitude.

When you appreciate both the big and small successes you have made, it helps you develop resilience during adversity.

When you are grateful for the achievements you have made, you will be more likely to embrace failure and see it as an opportunity to learn something new instead of seeing it as an obstacle. Even when you are not progressing fast enough, you can stay confident in your ability and know that you are still on track to achieve the goals that you have set.

Your resilience keeps you going when other individuals may have stopped trying and have given up, thereby helping you to attain higher success levels.

Be thankful for the things you have and more will come to you. If you keep your focus on the things that you lack, you will continue to lack and never have enough.

Gratitude brings about a growth mindset

You might go through a lot and learn some difficult lessons along the way before you become successful, and there might even be moments of self-doubt. It takes many years of dedication and hard work to get to the finish line, and sometimes we can even forget the reason we chose this path. Gratitude keeps your eyes on the destination.

When your focus is on the things you are grateful for, your drive and motivation increase significantly. You need to understand that you can succeed if you can keep pushing forward in whatever you want to do.

Gratitude brings about a growth mindset whereby you believe that your capabilities and skills are not predetermined and that there will be a significant difference if you put in effort. Gratitude makes us see the accomplishments we make as stepping stones on our path to achieving greater success.

When you appreciate the progress you are making, you have a higher likelihood of looking for opportunities for self-improvement and growth and embracing challenges. We set standards that are higher for ourselves and believe that we can achieve our dreams. This growth mindset brings us long-term success and fulfillment.

Gratitude can be a source of resilience and strength throughout your career. You look back at your journey with gratitude. You feel grateful every day for the skills and knowledge that help you in your career. You enjoy your work because you are aware of everybody and all the experiences that have helped you get to where you are today.

Allow gratitude to continue being a major part of your life and help you stay motivated, humble, and driven. It can help you reach your greatest potential. By embracing gratitude, you appreciate the successes that you have already achieved and also create room for more accomplishments in the future.

CHAPTER 8
Humility: An Individual's Greatest Strength

Humility is powerful. In fact, it brings success. Although many people consider humility a weakness, the reality is that it can be an individual's greatest strength. It opens us up to new perspectives and ideas. It also allows us to be more understanding and forgiving of others, and to be more empathetic and compassionate. Humility has the ability to make us successful in our professional and personal lives.

In our present world, everybody is trying to do their best to stand out and also be the best. And people can see humility as a disadvantage. But the reality is that humility involves acknowledging your limitations and weaknesses and being willing to learn new things from other individuals and improve yourself. This willingness to grow and willingness to be open can bring about greater satisfaction and success in both your professional and personal life.

Humility also makes it possible for you to form better relationships with other people. We are less likely to take criticism personally or to be defensive when we are humble. This makes it easier for people to work with us and it also makes us more approachable, thereby leading to better teamwork and collaboration. We will achieve our goals more effectively through these positive relationships.

Another good thing about humility is that it can lead to increased self-awareness. When you are humble, you have a high likelihood of reflecting on your own behavior as well as taking responsibility for your actions. This self-awareness makes it possible for us to make changes that are positive in our lives and it also helps us to grow as individuals.

Humility can give us a greater sense of contentment and peace. When you are humble, you are less likely to allow comparison and envy to take over you, and you have a high likelihood of appreciating the good in other individuals and being grateful for what you have. This can lead to more happiness and satisfaction in your life.

Humility is powerful and should not be underestimated. Whether it is in your professional or personal life, being humble can make you great, bring you happiness, increase your self-awareness, and make your relationships better. So, you need to learn to embrace humility and be a humble individual.

The Role of Humility In Success

For many individuals who are drawn to success, it's quite common for them to expect the boost in ego that comes when they accomplish their goals and other individuals notice that they have achieved their goals. We all understand that good feeling that comes when the work you have done is admired by other individuals. The problem that is associated with seeking that boost in ego is that an absence of humility usually gets in the way of success.

oo many individuals worry that when a person is humble, people look down on them. They fear that other individuals will not respect them and this will affect their success. Many individuals who are successful in their lives are some of the most humble people.

This is how they were able to achieve their goals with humility:

Successful individuals know when they are wrong

Although many individuals have the fear of failure when they are pursuing success, it is an important part of the process. Individuals usually learn more from their failures than they do from the successes they achieve. Embracing your failure and allowing yourself to learn from it requires an act of humility. You must acknowledge that you did wrong as it will help you learn how to perform better in the future.

A common obstacle to success is the inability to admit faults. Humble people are aware that no individual is perfect; they know that everybody makes mistakes. This makes it possible for these people to learn from the mistakes they have made and also act boldly to work on new things.

If you are so worried about people seeing you fail that you prevent yourself from ambitious pursuits, ambitious things will be far away from you and you will find it difficult to achieve ambitious things. You need to understand that people don't always get it right all the time. There will be times when people are going to see you get it wrong, but that shouldn't stop you from trying again. You need to try again until you do it and get it right.

Successful individuals are able to count on those around them

Humility is an important quality that you need to have because it makes people embrace you and not see you as a threat. You need the help of other individuals to achieve your goals; you cannot do it all alone. The best way to find individuals who will spend their time to help you achieve your goals is to treat other individuals with respect. If you are not humble, it will be hard for you to find people who will stay loyal to you and what you are working on.

Although you may think others will be impressed by your bravado, it will likely reduce their connection to you. Put an end to the arrogant behavior and show the individuals you work with that you have the utmost respect for them.

Humility pays, so you need to be humble.

ou have no idea of the limits of your abilities. Whether you are a successful individual or not, if you continue pushing, you will make yourself rich and it may even spread to the people around you.

Successful individuals do not think less of themselves

Humility is not when you think less of yourself; it has to do with thinking of yourself less. Many individuals have the habit of thinking about how other individuals will perceive them and they try to control the perception.

When individuals learn to be humble, a lot of energy and time is freed up because this non-productive habit does not take up their thoughts. With all that extra energy and time, you will be able to keep your thoughts on what to do to further your goals and handle any challenges that show up along the way.

It takes complex thinking and creativity to solve problems on the path to success. A clear brain is needed for this, so don't fill your mind with thoughts that are irrelevant and centered on your ego. You will likely end up becoming more likeable when you stop worrying too much about whether or not other individuals see you the way you want them to see you.

Successful individuals are open to ideas

Any individual who is hoping to be successful must be open to new ideas. The path that leads to success is not always a straightforward one. Staying open to new ideas is important, as it helps you find innovative ways to achieve your goals. Arrogance usually stands in the way of open-mindedness. A lot of individuals are very certain that they know how to achieve their goals, so they make the mistake of not trying other options and being creative.

You need to have a sense of humility in the plans you make as you work towards achieving your goal. You need to understand that you may need to change some things at some point, and you don't have to feel bad about that. It is okay. It doesn't mean the plan you have made is not a good one; it just means that you are working towards a purpose that is challenging and also rewarding.

When you start your company, you may not know how big the company will become. You are hopeful that you will become successful, but you know that you will have to stay open to new ideas, looking for the best opportunities, and expanding. This mindset is what helped you grow to the current revenues you have.

CHAPTER 9
Vision: A Bridge To The Future

Are you aware that a clear vision can help you create massive success in your life?

Having sight without vision is the only thing that is worse than being blind. Improve your life with your vision today. Be consistent, bold, and creative.

At some point or the other in our lives, we ask ourselves these questions: Why are we here in the world? Where should we be in life? Every one of us has a purpose for why we are here, but what gives our purpose direction is vision.

What do you understand by vision?

Vision can be defined as an act of anticipating what may or will happen. It directs us and gives us a glimpse of our life to make our purpose and goals a reality. It is a mental image of the future you want for yourself and the ability to plan that future with wisdom.

A vision connects your present to the future you desire; it is like a bridge. It is a goal to create a way for positive changes and it is a dream that exists deep within your heart. It is a call to do an extraordinary thing and improve yourself and not just a view of the big picture. A vision gives you courage, determination, and hope. You can do whatever is required to get to the top if you are focused on your vision.

You need to have a clear vision for your life in order to have a full understanding of where you should be in life. So, when you fully understand that vision brings clarity of purpose, your life will become more meaningful and simpler. Having purpose and vision is important as you will make better decisions, which ultimately creates the life you desire.

It is not easy to find your purpose. People will keep telling you what you are good at, what careers you should explore, and how best to live your life, but it can be chaotic and confusing at times. But once you find out your purpose by yourself and then write your vision down, your life becomes less complex and becomes simple. Society has confused many people and made them believe that success comes from how busy they are. So, a lot of people believe that the busier they are, the more important and successful they will become, which is not usually the case. Once you know your purpose, your life becomes clearer and more focused because you know what you want and are working towards it. When you find your purpose and also create your vision, your life will start taking shape. Remember to enjoy the ride.

We are all moving somewhere in life. You either have a vision and know where you are taking yourself to or you just allow life to happen to you and take you anywhere if you have no vision. A few individuals end up where they want to be on purpose. Those are the individuals with a vision and a dream that is clearly defined.

Successful people may face challenges as well. But one thing is certain: they have a clear vision and dream, and they also have the courage to take action. This dramatically increases their chances of becoming successful. If you don't aim for anything, you will not achieve anything. This is the reality.

Professional players are highly trained and skilled, so they usually make the game look so easy. It is possible to have highly skilled and trained players playing the game, but accomplishing nothing after wearing themselves out.

Sadly, many highly trained and skilled business owners are not reaching their full potential because they have failed to clearly identify their dreams. They are moving around in circles and not going anywhere. The problem is that they have no vision to guide them in the decisions they make daily. So, they try doing things urgently, but never really get anything done.

The worst thing that can happen to you is to have sight without vision. Many people suffer losses because they lack vision.

They live their lives without restraint and give their attention and time to whatever screams the loudest instead of spending time doing the things that will move them forward in life.

For an individual who owns a business, the backbone of their business plan should be structured around the passions and dreams that they have. You can measure the progress you are making toward your goal after you have clearly defined your life purpose.

Defining your life purpose requires a process of self-evaluation and reflection, and this takes work. But you will enjoy the benefits if you can clearly state what you want out of life.

If a leader doesn't have a vision to guide their day-to-day decisions, they will find themselves going nowhere.

So, do you have a vision for business and your life? If you have a vision, it's a good thing. You need to break it down into action steps that you will perform every day. Have you done that yet? Are you living your life according to your purpose?

You can create a path to success if you have a vision. So, have you started visualizing what you want to achieve personally and professionally?

Importance of Vision

Although it is good to value the present, staying focused on your future is also important. You need to take time out to think about what you really want to become and what you want to have in some months and years from now. For this to be possible, you need to have a vision that is meaningful and clear.

One problem that causes individuals to get stuck and not progress is that they lack a vision and good planning. If you notice that you are one of the people who don't have a clear vision and plan, you need to make a mindset shift and start making changes that will get you started on your journey towards success.

Here are the reasons why every one of us should have a vision, whether it is for our business, career, or personal purposes:

A vision shows you the steps to take

We often believe that an individual must learn in school, complete their studies, get a job, and then think about retirement after years of working. This is the pattern that appears to be stuck in our minds. You can change things and become an improved version of yourself by having clarity of vision.

You can begin by asking yourself these questions:

Where will I be in five years' time?

How much money should I have as my savings after retiring?

How will the money I saved be used in the future?

The above questions are just samples of what you can ask yourself to know what kind of life you desire to have. You will find it easy to determine which steps to take once you have a vision.

A vision provides you with a sense of direction

When you are walking in a dark room, trying to find something, it will be difficult to find that thing. This is why vision is important in life. Vision gives you a sense of direction and a better path is created for a better life. For example, if you aim to become a very successful entrepreneur and you want to achieve it within three years, then it is important that you have a vision that is clear so that you understand everything you need to do to achieve that goal. These things can include coming up with creative concepts, reducing your expenses, working harder, and increasing your knowledge of business management.

Vision will create more mistakes for you

Every one of us makes mistakes, and they are inevitable in life. There will be times in our lives when we will encounter bumps and rocky roads no matter how hard we try to make things perfect. We will experience times when we feel alone and neglected. At these times, we feel that when we try to prove ourselves to other individuals, we are then judged and rejected. We may also make bad decisions because we don't plan but just allow things to happen according to chance. When you have a vision, you will have a proper way to handle specific goals. You will know the right approach to take to move forward. Once you are aware of what your purpose is, you will easily achieve what you want to achieve.

Every successful person who wants to create something first starts with a vision, so you must begin by creating your vision if you desire to be successful.

Factors that Hinder Vision

A variety of factors can hinder an individual's vision to become successful. We all need to be aware of these factors so that we can follow our vision.

Let us take a look at the factors:

1. Imitating other people's lives

When a person hears a story that inspires them, it should motivate them to create an improved life for themselves and not make them go ahead to copy it without making any improvements in their life. Everybody has unique abilities and talents. Therefore, we all are capable of becoming unusual and unique in our own ways. Do not allow other people's lives to dictate how you live your life.

2. The distraction factor

Both big and small distractions surround us. Even when you are at home, different elements and things can distract you from achieving the result you dream of achieving. Although, you may have ideas and a plan on how your vision will be achieved, some other things like hobbies, games, fun events, television, and others can affect the plans. If you allow these things to distract your plans and focus, all that you have arranged will be wasted. You need to learn to face your responsibility, stay focused on the plan, and do your best to achieve the results that you desire.

3. The fear factor

Dreaming big can be inspiring, but it can also be scary. Fear stops people from having big dreams. Do not allow fear to hinder you from doing great things when you have a vision of what you want to achieve. When fear begins to weigh you down, it makes you lose the motivation and enthusiasm to pursue your dreams. You need to learn how to be courageous enough to face any challenges that may come your way and overcome fear.

4. Failed expectations

When expectations are stated in positive ways, they can be good. However, they can also cause negative effects. When you set high expectations and you don't achieve them, it can result in a decrease in your self-esteem and self-confidence. That is why you need to set your expectations in such a way that they are not too high. Prepare yourself for failures and stay determined to improve.

How Vision Helps You Achieve Success

Vision can help you succeed in these ways:

Vision leads you to your desired future

If you lack vision, you will not know the way to achieve your dreams. On the other hand, different directions can sometimes be offered to you by life, but the number of roads available doesn't matter. One important question to ask yourself is: Which way should you go? When you have a vision, you will know where to go. You will easily get to your target destination once vision drives you. You will also come up with techniques that are useful that you can use for your personal development and business. The vision you have today is your future reality.

Vision helps you think forward

We should be thinking forward when we create the visions we have for our lives. What moving forward means is to be true to yourself on the goal you want to achieve without holding back. You need to know what you really want as it will help you know the right direction to take. You need to know that every successful venture begins with a vision. Every innovative change and creative idea starts from the mind, so stretching your imagination to achieve your vision is important. Take time to make improvements to your life by embracing values and learning new things. You may experience some rejections as well as some distractions, but rejections and distractions are things that everybody experiences. Believing in your vision's beauty is important.

Vision helps to create the habits you have

Once you realize what you want, vision does many things for you. It also creates your habits. Your to-do list is created and it helps you know what to do, and this will then create your habits over time. Any individual with a vision of achieving a particular thing will eventually create habits that will get them ready for that vision.

If you want to prepare for your vision, you might take time to read business books for 1 hour every morning, to help you understand how to run a successful business. And when you get to the office, you might create time to listen to business interviews online. You can listen to other individuals who are already successful entrepreneurs, to learn the things they did that made them successful. You can even decide to attend seminars to learn from other entrepreneurs firsthand.

Vision can help you control your world

These norms may be in your mind: to get a degree, get a job, and have a family. While this is not wrong, this generalization is capable of keeping you locked up for your thinking that these things are what are the most important things that people need in their lives. True happiness begins within you, not from external things. Vision will help you learn to control your world to achieve the things you want to achieve. You need to embrace your uniqueness, go all out, and allow yourself to shine. The vision you have will take care of it since you are willing and ready to take action and consistently put in the work.

Vision can foster self-belief and provide freedom

A vision is capable of helping you grow as an individual or as an entrepreneur looking to achieve success. It has the ability to increase your self-belief and help you transform into an improved version of yourself. Ensure that you create the biggest vision for your life because what you believe is what you will become.

Vision helps you make wise use of your time

There is a connection between our vision and how we spend our time. If you have a vision that is important to you, you will spend time pursuing it. This is a really simple principle that many people often make complicated. For instance, if you make up your mind that you want to be the Employee of the Month in your workplace, you might stop spending time partying after you leave the office. Instead, you might start getting more sleep at night and spending more time on your work to align with your vision.

To achieve your goal as well as your purpose, the amount of time you spend will determine the actions you take to achieve your vision. It is the same thing that any disciplined athlete does when it comes to sports. A great athlete is admired not for his skills, but for his discipline. This is because his discipline shows his skills. He knows that he needs to discipline himself to win the championship. So, he dedicates himself to a strict workout routine every day to get himself prepared for the mental and physical part of the game. Going to the gym early and also engaging in training can help to prepare him and help him win the championship.

This shows that the most important resource we have is time, as it is a non-renewable resource. When time is wasted, you cannot get that time back to use tomorrow, because tomorrow is not even guaranteed. People, opportunities, and money can always come back into your life later, but lost time is gone forever and can never be recovered. Vision helps you use your time wisely so that you don't waste it.

Vision can help you make changes

Let yourself know that you can do what you want to do, and you will do it. Motivating yourself this way can make things easier. Most people have the problem of caring too much about the things that other individuals say. This is quite common with a lot of people. When you allow yourself to be controlled by the opinions of other individuals, it becomes hard to see improvements. Your vision is capable of awakening your senses. It is a force that is capable of pulling you away from unhealthy habits and distractions. When you focus on it, you allow yourself to discover the changes that you need to improve and you embrace those changes.

Vision makes you take action

Have you ever sat down alone and asked yourself the question about what you can do that will get you closer to your dreams? Your willingness to take action has something to do with the vision that you have. When your mind is overtaken by your vision, you will learn to get over your fears and create a better future for your business. You become more productive when you have a vision. However, when you are hesitating with your vision, you will miss out on accomplishing something great. To accomplish something great, you need to have a vision.

Vision shines a light on your path

The results you desire can be achieved with the vision of your life. No matter how dark and tough your journey can be, your vision is capable of shining a light on your path during the dark times. The key is to welcome every challenge that you face on the way to your destination. So, instead of running away from challenges, you need to embrace the challenges and be positive about them. As you get to understand more about your vision, you will be able to create harmony in achieving your dreams. You need to keep moving ahead and staying focused on your vision.

Vision can stop you from making unnecessary mistakes

When you have a vision, you can make a calculated assessment that will help you achieve your goals. It can make you vigilant, passionate, and alert. This way, you prevent some mistakes that may happen. When you focus on the things that can go right instead of the things that can go wrong, you are making it possible for things to fall into place.

Vision selects the friends we make

In the same way, vision chooses the direction we go in our lives, it also chooses our friends and those we spend time with. People usually spend time with those individuals with a vision and who are disciplined when it comes to their vision. We usually do not associate ourselves with individuals who have no idea where they are going in life. Even if you hang out with them, it won't be for long because time is being wasted. The truth is that it is frustrating and mentally draining to be around individuals who do not know where they want to be in life or how they will get there.

Once you have a vision, you will start separating yourself from individuals who are not in alignment with your vision and aligning yourself with those who fit your vision. This is one great thing about vision. Nobody can fulfill their purpose alone, because a person's purpose is bigger than them and that is how it is meant to be. Your purpose will benefit you and also create room for other individuals to learn and grow in your vision and purpose. So, when people say that they are self-made millionaires, do not allow the propaganda to fool you because nobody is completely a self-made millionaire. Anybody who has achieved financial success achieved success because of their ability to share their vision and surround themselves with individuals willing to invest in their vision. You should have friends who should be able to add value to your vision and purpose and help you with the fulfillment. Once you have a full understanding of your vision, it will attract individuals who are willing to invest in it, if they see that you are honest and open.

You can use your vision to influence and lead other individuals

One remarkable purpose of success is to inspire others. You know that you have grown into a better person when you gain a lot of knowledge from your experiences and visions. A strong foundation that has the ability to make your dream a reality is created by your vision. Allow your vision to be a symbol of hope and an established legacy for other individuals.

Your vision can help you win big

One important thing that vision does is that it becomes a source of motivation for you on your journey to success. You need to understand that you learn and you win as you move ahead. Success will come your way if you believe in your vision and in yourself.

A clear vision has the ability to enhance business and your life.

So, if you are ready to kickstart the process of following your vision, you need to ask yourself these questions:

What exactly do you want to achieve?

What is your reason for that?

What benefits will you get from doing it?

What negative results will come up if you don't do it?

Be committed to setting aside some time to honestly answer these questions. The answers might surprise you.

It is important that you form the right habits that align with your vision. Habits are things that individuals do every day. They do it most of the time without being conscious of it, but successful people are conscious of their habits.

Create and stick to habits that move you closer to your purpose and vision. You need to understand that how you spend your resources, energy, and time can move you one step closer to where you want to be. We will talk more about habits in the next chapter.

CHAPTER 10
Habit

Good habits have the ability to improve the relationship you have with customers. Customers need high-quality customer care and excellent services. Being knowledgeable about customer care won't make you an excellent customer care service provider or a great sales manager.

When you use your personality and go the extra mile, you demonstrate excellent customer care. Using your personality includes using your body language, gestures, and words to inspire an individual to see the product's beauty through your habits. Your habits will determine the quality of service you provide to customers, as the habits will either make you give your customers a positive experience or a negative experience which will stay in their memory. If people have a positive experience with you, they will remember the service you provided them and the positive experience. This will in turn increase your success.

You need to know the following:

Small steps can generate big rewards

We usually expect big changes in our behaviour and we also set challenging goals. For example, you might say you will wake up at 4 am, or make 20 million in the first year of your business. The reality of things is that the formation of new habits or change is small and this requires incremental steps that are repeated to take hold.

When you have a goal that you want to achieve, you may get disheartened when you don't make any significant progress toward that goal that you want to achieve. This affects your desire to repeat the behavior that the brain needs to create new habits. So, what can you do about this?

You need to break your goals into smaller habits that you can achieve habitually and easily. The brain releases adrenaline, the energy hormone, and dopamine, the feel-good hormone when you achieve goals. An upward spiral is created where you feel motivated and you also have the energy to do more.

So, if you have a target of 20 million, you can break the goal down into smaller goals and work on each small goal until you complete them all and reach your target.

Good habits open the doors to new opportunities

According to the law of karma, you get back what you do to others. Good habits help individuals to be successful in business and life. Bad habits and corrupt practices are great at destroying a brand and business. Good habits and a good personality attract many opportunities and also create a powerful brand. The way people interact and connect has changed as a result of social media. Social media has made many individuals excel in their lives and careers. These days, big organizations ask to know your social media accounts so they can see how you interact with other individuals online through your posts, photos, and comments. Organizations believe that your social media accounts can show them who you are. Employment opportunities or business opportunities can be missed as a result of bad habits displayed when using social media. Your behavior is not only seen when you meet people physically but your behavior is also seen from the things you share on social media.

Many successful individuals have good habits, and they are aware that habits are powerful tools that shape their lives, both professionally and personally. An individual's habit is a behavior that is made automatic through repetition. Habits are performed without even thinking about what you are doing. Checking your phone when you wake up in the morning and brushing your teeth are habits. You form habits in your life when your brain recognizes a pattern and creates neural pathways that make performing the behavior in the future easier.

One good thing about habits is that you will find them beneficial if you cultivate good ones, like being more organized or doing regular exercise. However, bad habits, such as smoking or procrastination can negatively affect your relationships, health, and productivity. If you are worried about some bad habits, you need to worry no more because bad habits can be changed to good ones when you put in the required effort and dedication.

Reminders

Behavioral scientists say that when you come up with a routine that weaves the new behavior you desire into your daily life to increase the repetition of the behavior, it may become a default response one day as a result of the repetition and then a habit. This plan requires routine and consistency. You also need a reminder to do it.

This reminds you to behave in a particular way when a certain situation presents itself. It can be achieved by adding the new behaviors you desire into existing habits. This creates an easily repeatable behavior that is achievable and enables you to create a positive upward spiral to fulfill a goal that is bigger and more important.

Once you have repeated the behavior enough, the brain gets used to it and it becomes a new habit, thereby moving to the unconscious from the conscious.

What are the goals you are working on at the moment that you need to break down into smaller goals? How can you create mental cues or plans to make sure that the behavior you desire can be easily recalled and acted upon based on cues present in your environment? You can start small and be on your way to forming the habits that will make you successful.

CHAPTER 11
The Role Of Creativity And Innovation In Success

Creativity and innovation are important for an individual or organization's growth and success. To be successful, you need to create value for your customers and also for yourself.

You can do this by identifying opportunities, getting problems diagnosed, and also developing valuable commercial solutions.

When it comes to entrepreneurship, creativity and innovation form the bedrock. They impact your income and your wealth.

While creating a business that becomes successful and then sustaining the business requires more than innovation and creativity, these two factors are very important.

What is Creativity?

The cognitive activity that leads to unconventional or novel ideas that have not been previously used or known is referred to as creativity. Useful and original ideas are generated through this process. The raw material used in innovation is creativity.

What is Innovation?

Innovation is the process whereby new ideas are used to create new value. Although innovation is dependent upon the ideas that flow from creativity as well as creativity itself, innovation is not just about having creative and new ideas. The ideas must be commercially viable, they must be valuable, and they must also be implemented to create new value.

Innovation has to do with understanding the process of creativity and managing it, and then transforming the ideas into commercial reality with the resources available.

The Relationship between Creativity and Innovation

There is a connection between creativity and innovation. They are an important part of the entrepreneurial process as well as the keys to growth and long-term success.

Innovation and creativity are highly interdependent and interactive activities that are at the heart of the creation process of value and your ability to capture this value's share.

Given the importance of innovation and creativity to the realization of the dreams and aspirations of the entrepreneur, there must be a proactive management of both activities. If you want to secure your future, they shouldn't be left to wishful thinking or chance.

The following are involved when it comes to the management and development of organizational and personal creativity:

Building knowledge, competency, and creativity.

Managing mindsets as well as dispensing with the major misconceptions that innovation and creativity are surrounded by.

Building management systems for innovation that have the capability of transforming creative ideas into commercial outcomes.

Establishing an environment that maximizes intrinsic motivation and supports creativity.

Creativity is the idea source that flows into innovation, where it creates value that increases income and wealth. A single breakthrough idea is not all that is needed, but creating an environment that gives creativity room to flourish and one where ideas are used effectively in the innovation process.

Your business will be left behind if there is no appropriate environment that will encourage new ideas and the right process to commercialize the ideas.

Your competitive advantage will be eroded by competitors that have more aggressive growth aspirations, jeopardizing your future wealth and income.

Ensure that you build innovation and creativity into your business' DNA if you want to make sure that you don't lose the competitive race. Innovation and creativity result in a high rate of success in organizations. Educational institutions and traditional companies usually prize intelligence as the factor that is the most important in problem-solving. This preference might have been from ease instead of best practices.

Creativity can be difficult to identify, and intelligence is easier to measure and manage than creativity. The company will experience improvement when creative thinking is made a priority, encouragement is provided to creatively solve problems, and positive feedback is received.

Attaining New Heights

Innovation and creativity can help your business to get to new heights of productivity, process improvement, product value, marketing, productivity, internal harmony, and marketing success. The creative process can result in novel concepts and ideas. This is true especially when conventional convergent thought complements the divergent thinking it requires.

When a diverse cross-functional team seeks to innovate by implementing creative ideas, their work will be more flexible and effective, and they will work with a greater sense of unity. From minor office changes to product designs that are ahead of the competition, any new improvement that is made to your business is innovation. This is a process that doesn't happen only once.

Continued innovative use of creative ideas and a dedication to creativity are capable of driving the growth of a business impressively. It takes comfort in the encouragement and approach of the process. And why not get comfortable with the availability of these kinds of benefits?

Do you think that your organization innovates frequently? Could it be that you may have been innovating without even realizing it? Does your organization encourage and promote creativity? How does your organization do that? How can you start encouraging innovation and creativity in your organization?

CONCLUSION

In this book, we have discussed what you need to know to become successful and influential. So, you need to get to work and start working on your expertise. Don't worry if you are not the best on the first day. Build until you get to the point you want to get to. You will be amazed by how much you will grow in a year's time if you consistently spend time every day to invest in your growth.

If your business is online, you need to spend time trying out different marketing hacks. When you try it for a year, you will see what works for you and what doesn't.

Once you have discovered what works and what doesn't, ensure that you continue doing more of what works for you and avoid doing what doesn't work. Instead of allowing the fear of mistakes to stop you from trying, learn from the mistakes that you have already made and move on with your life.

Effort is required when it comes to building your expertise. And your expertise will pave the way to your success. Things may not appear easy at first, but you need to try. Don't just wait for success without doing anything to achieve it. Understand that doing nothing means that you are blocking yourself from becoming successful. So, you need to stop blocking yourself from trying to do the things that are required for your success.

What do procrastination, bad days, roadblocks, and failures have in common? They all exist in your head. You may be so used to roadblocks that your first reaction will always be to find the workaround. You may even do some weird things just to go over obstacles.

If you realize that you had a bad sleep the night before, the solution to your problem is easy. You just need to go to sleep earlier that night. You will feel as if that bad day never happened. Don't allow any external force to block your success. You need to remove the mental barrier in your head. Change your perspective if there is anything you need to change about yourself.

You can't become successful if you don't do anything at all. Don't think that you will get a big financial reward for doing nothing. Energy and time are required to build something if you want to be successful. Many of the successful people are creators. Devoting your life to being a creator will help you see what it takes to achieve success. But this takes consistent effort and time.

You may just want to put on the TV and turn off your brain, but to get the kind of results that successful people get, you need to do what they do.

Being successful depends on you. If you are not willing to do the work that success requires, you won't accomplish great things.

So, if you want to be successful and influential, you need to start building something. And if you don't want to be successful and influential but only like the idea of it, you can relax and watch others become successful while you continue daydreaming. The choice is yours.

If you decide that success is not your thing, I hope that you will find fulfillment in whatever you do and have no regrets years from now.

You need to stop looking for the easy way out, start creating better goals, start working on building your expertise, and start taking action.

Ensure that you continue to innovate, as the market is quite competitive. When ideation is concerned, do your best to push the envelope.

Remember that building relationships is important for success. You cannot achieve great things alone. Develop good habits that will help you achieve success and put an end to the bad habits that keep you down. You can start by replacing the bad habits with good habits. Use positive self-talk and not negative self-talk. Positive self-talk builds you up, but negative self-talk destroys you. You need to surround yourself with the right people that can help you become successful. Spend time with people who understand vision and have a vision for their lives. Having a vision for your life will help you make wise use of your time and not waste it.

Understand that power and influence will help you accomplish great things. Informational power is short-term and does not necessarily build credibility or influence.

For instance, the manager of a project may have all the necessary information for a particular project, thereby giving the project manager informational power. However, it can be difficult for an individual to keep informational power for long, as they will eventually release the information. This strategy should not be a long-term one.

Connection power creates influence by proxy and this usually comes from solid networking skills. This type of power can be attained when you gain favor and you are a resource to people.

If you want to reach someone and I have a connection with that person, that means I have connection power. That is a kind of politics because individuals who employ this power usually build important coalitions with other people.

Coercive power may have short-term effects, but this power can also lead to unengaged and unhappy employees which impacts the retention of employees. Leaders need to have a full understanding of the different types of power available and also use the powers in the right way.

Effective leaders should be aware of the different types of power and they should be able to use these powers in different situations. Being aware of the right type of power to use in different situations is a skill that one acquires with practice and experience.

Leaders can become more successful when they possess the ability to use different types of power.

Remember that an effective leader is aware of how to use the different types of power to solve any situation at hand. Therefore, leaders don't only need to understand the different types of power, but they also need to understand the best ways to use them to achieve the best for the team and the entire company. A great leader combines both internal and external power and also strikes a balance between influence and genuine authority.

Passion and persistence are important for success. Entrepreneurship and business development should be built out of love. You will achieve great success if you build great relationships with people. Understand that it may not be easy as you experience failures and setbacks along the way, but if you are persistent, you will eventually find success and fulfillment.